Kate Scharff, ~~M.S.W.~~
and Lisa Herrick, Ph.D.

Navigating Emotional Currents in Collaborative Divorce

A Guide to Enlightened Team Practice

**Foreword by
Pauline H. Tesler**

**Defending Liberty
Pursuing Justice**

SECTION OF
FAMILY LAW

Cover design by ABA Publishing.

Printed in the United States of America.

14 13 12 11   5 4 3 2

Library of Congress Cataloging-in-Publication Data is on file with the Library of Congress.

Navigating Emotional Currents in Collaborative Divorce: A Guide to Enlightened Team Practice
Kate Scharff and Lisa Herrick
ISBN: 978-1-61632-074-4

Discounts are available for books ordered in bulk. Special consideration is given to state bars, CLE programs, and other bar-related organizations. Inquire at Book Publishing, ABA Publishing, American Bar Association, 321 North Clark Street, Chicago, Illinois 60654-7598.

www.ababooks.org

KATE'S DEDICATION

For my father, David E. Scharff, MD
For his support, encouragement, and inspiration from the beginning

LISA'S DEDICATION

For my parents, Bill and Jeannette Herrick, for my children, Nick and Sarah, and for my husband, Drey, with love. I feel grateful every day that you are my family.

CONTENTS

KATE AND LISA'S
ACKNOWLEDGMENTS

We want to start by thanking all the visionaries in the field of Collaborative Practice from whom we have had the privilege of learning, especially Stu Webb, Pauline Tesler, Ron Ousky, Susan Gamache, Sue Brunsting, and Peggy Thompson. Peggy has been a wonderfully generous teacher; our telephone supervision group with her has become a linchpin in our ongoing learning. The International Academy of Collaborative Practice is a powerhouse of an institution; it is our professional North Star.

Next, we want to acknowledge all of our beloved Collaborative colleagues in the Greater Washington, D.C., area with whom it has been a pleasure to work, particularly our fellow founding members of the DC Academy of Collaborative Professionals (DCACP), our co-trainers at the Collaborative Practice Training Institute (CPTI), and our co-coaches in the Collaborative Mental Health Professionals Group. Space limitations prevent us from naming you all, but we would be remiss if we didn't specifically mention certain people on whose support, expertise, humor, and friendship we draw on a near-daily basis: Lonnie Broussard, Adele D'Ari, Susie Eckstein, Francie Fite, Karen Keyes, Margie Hofberg, Michael McHugh, Frank Morrison, Lisa Schenkel, Paul Smollar, David Tyson, Debbie May, Sarah Zimmerman, and Carl Mitlehner. An extra hug for Barb Burr, Karen Freed, Andrea Hirsch, Mary Pence, Sue Soler, and Jan White—great friends who found time in their busy schedules to read our manuscript at various phases and offer invaluable feedback and advice.

Our hats go off to our friends on the DC Metro Protocols Committee. Your gargantuan efforts have resulted in a thoroughly helpful living document that is sure to play a part in the ongoing development of the field.

Linda Ravdin encouraged us from the beginning of this project, guided us, and tolerated our ongoing anxieties with patience and humor. Thanks to the ABA for giving us this opportunity, and particularly to Amelia Stone, Jeff Salyards, and Joe Booth for their helpful responsiveness to our steady stream of questions and requests. A special shout-out to Ellen Murphy for designing many of the graphics in this book, and to Rebecca Cruz, Shanel Espreo, and Ewelina Kotalma for all their administrative support on this and other projects.

Finally, we want to thank the families with whom we have worked since embarking on this Collaborative journey. We have learned most of what we know from you. Your trust, creativity, courage, and commitment continue to inspire us and infuse the pages of this book.

KATE'S ACKNOWLEDGMENTS

I wish to thank my colleagues, teachers, and supervisors at the International Psychotherapy Institute (IPI), especially the faculty of IPI's Metro Washington Center—Bonnie Eisenberg, Sheila Hill, Rachel Kaplan, Mona Mendelson, Jane Prelinger, and Patrizia Pallaro. My Collaborative work is an application of all I learned at my first professional home.

My parents and sibs—Isabel, David, Jill, Zoe, Xanthe, Daniel, Nell, and Doug—are an ongoing source of loving encouragement. Thanks especially to my sister Nell—for always helping me to get out of my own way, and for a million other things. Ewelina Kotalma has been a critical member of our clan since coming to live with us six years ago. She keeps my life running. Bill Pratt has been a much-needed cheerleader over this past year, and distracted me when I needed it. Maggie Simpson is a great friend in all ways. My amazing children Chloe and Ben—it's a pleasure watching you grow as the insightful, funny, loving, creative, and generous people you are. I'm grateful to you for tolerating my professional absences and preoccupations, and for teaching me all my most important lessons. I'm proud to be your mother.

Finally, I want to thank my dear friend and closest colleague, Lisa Herrick. She gently but firmly nudges me into new professional areas, and I'm always grateful. Working with her—whether we're teaching, writing, or on a Collaborative team—often feels like improvised ballet. Her insights, energy, unflagging support, and sense of humor keep me going. I feel lucky for our professional partnership every day.

LISA'S ACKNOWLEDGMENTS

My family, my friends, and my colleagues have filled my life with humor, wisdom, and love. For all of this I want to thank my siblings: Jon and Pearlyn; Michael and Shelley.

My friends: Nancy, Jude, Annie, Carolyn, Amy, Naomi, Barbara, Molly, Deb, Adele, Jane, and Dan.

And thank you to Mary Lanman, who helped me become my best self.

Finally, I want to thank Kate Scharff, who pulled me into this book and then infused our work with her insight, energy, and genuine wish to give something valuable to our field and our community. She inspires me, makes me laugh, and surprises me regularly with her capacity to see the world at its most confusing moments in a way that makes everything come clear.

ABOUT THE AUTHORS

 **Kate Scharff, MSW** is a clinical social worker with over 20 years of experience working with individuals, couples, and families. She received her graduate degree from the Columbia University School of Social Work and her psychotherapy training at the Institute for Child, Adolescent and Family Studies in New York City and the International Psychotherapy Institute in Chevy Chase, Maryland, where she is on the faculty. Ms. Scharff is a founding member and president-elect of the D.C. Academy of Collaborative Professionals, serves on the faculty of the Collaborative Practice Training Institute, and is a co-founder and principal of the Collaborative Practice Center of Greater Washington. She is a member of several other professional organizations, including the International Academy of Collaborative Professionals, the Maryland Collaborative Practice Council, and the Montgomery County Divorce Roundtable (of which she is President-Elect). Ms. Scharff has taught widely on psychodynamic psychotherapy, divorce, and Collaborative Practice, and is the author of several articles, book chapters, and the book *Therapy Demystified: An Insider's Guide to Getting the Right Help* (Marlowe and Co., 2005). Ms. Scharff maintains a private practice in individual and couple psychotherapy, mediation, parenting coordination, and Collaborative Practice, both in Washington, D.C., and in Bethesda, Maryland.

www.katescharff.com

Lisa Herrick, Ph.D. is a licensed clinical psychologist and a founding member of the West Falls Psychotherapy Group in Falls Church, VA. She has worked with couples, families, and children for over 20 years in her clinical practice. She is a former President of the D.C. Academy of Collaborative Professionals (DCACP) and currently serves on their board. She is also a member of Collaborative Professionals of Northern Virginia (CPNV). Dr. Herrick has completed over 65 Collaborative cases on multidisciplinary teams and has worked as a Collaborative Coach and as a Child Specialist. She is a founding member of the Collaborative Practice Training Institute (CPTI) and offers trainings throughout the country in working with high conflict parents and in Collaborative Practice. In August 2010, she opened, with several Collaborative colleagues, the Collaborative Practice Center of Greater Washington, a place where attorneys, mental health professionals, and financial experts can share office space and work together to advance Collaborative Practice in the Washington, D.C., area.

www.lisaherrick.com

FOREWORD

Kate Scharff and Lisa Herrick have written an extraordinary treatise, *Navigating Emotional Currents in Collaborative Divorce: A Guide to Enlightened Team Practice*. This is the book the Collaborative community has been waiting for: an accessible, practical grounding for Collaborative lawyers (as well as financial and allied professionals) in how to bring to our conflict resolution work something of the psychological understandings and skills that we so admire and envy in our mental health colleagues. For mental health professionals who are curious about Collaborative Practice, this book will introduce you to a way of applying your existing psychotherapeutic skills in a new field.

In the late 1990s, I had the privilege of working together with Bay Area psychologist Peggy Thompson and social worker Nancy Ross to integrate the divorce coaching and financial services team model they had originated with Collaborative Law, which by then was my primary mode of working with divorcing clients. Out of that joint effort emerged interdisciplinary team Collaborative Divorce Practice as we know it today, a model that has swept the field of family law not only in North America, but also in Europe, Australia, Israel, and elsewhere. The value for clients and their children of interdisciplinary Collaborative professional team service delivery is incalculable. A broader, deeper, and more durable kind of conflict resolution becomes possible when the professional helpers take the time to learn the art and craft of teamwork, and to build the trust relationships that are the ground for effective Collaborative service delivery.

The challenge in team service delivery lies in the need for divorce professionals who have previously worked with their clients primarily as "lone rangers" to learn how to share the

Collaborative sandbox. However skillful we may be as lawyers, mental health professionals, or financial advisors, we are all beginners at interdisciplinary teamwork. Every interaction between two or more people on a Collaborative divorce case provides banana peels to slip on, sore toes to step upon, rabbit holes to fall into. Collaborative teamwork may involve regular communications among as many as seven team members, multiplying the opportunities for missteps geometrically. At the same time, Collaborative teams also provide abundant opportunities for professionals to learn together what works, what does not, and why. Until now, the process of learning skillful teamwork has been somewhat hit or miss, depending on the personality and dedication of individuals and the degree to which the trainers who have taught them about Collaborative Practice have grasped the complex challenges of interdisciplinary teamwork and have developed effective ways to teach about it.

Now, at last, there is a deskbook that both beginning and experienced Collaborative professionals can turn to for a clear, user-friendly, yet sophisticated grounding in the dynamics of interdisciplinary team collaboration. Scharff and Herrick begin with the basics about human behavior during divorce, both functional and dysfunctional, that every Collaborative professional needs to understand in order to make the shift from adversarial legal dispute resolution into the more nuanced world of human conflict resolution. These concepts are presented clearly and straightforwardly without jargon, and are anchored in teaching stories drawn from the authors' extensive experience in Collaborative Divorce Practice. These practical illustrations of snafus in team practice and the emotional dynamics that drive them make the material immediately accessible even to lawyers and financial consultants who may have had little prior exposure to psychodynamic concepts. Practice tips and checklists derived from the theoretical material make it possible for Collaborative professionals to read the book today and implement new skills at tomorrow's Collaborative meeting. Particularly impressive is the authors' smooth and skillful exploration of how the dysfunctional behaviors we struggle to manage in our difficult clients can trigger equally dysfunctional behaviors in their professional helpers, and how the dysfunctional patterns of our clients' failing marriages can be mirrored in dysfunctional dynamics on the professional team.

These people know what they are talking about, and they present it simply and compellingly. This book is the first of its kind, and it has transformative potential. Every lawyer—every professional—who is serious about this work ought to read it, and Collaborative practice groups that aim to foster effective team practice would surely benefit from using this book as a resource.

Pauline H. Tesler
Collaborative lawyer and trainer
Co-founder and first president of the International
Academy of Collaborative Professionals
Author of *Collaborative Law: Achieving Effective
Resolution in Divorce without Litigation*
Recipient of the ABA's first Lawyer as Problem Solver award
teslercollaboration@lawtsf.com

Introduction: Navigating the Collaborative River Above and Below the Surface

Who We Are

We are a clinical social worker and a psychologist, both psychotherapists with over 20 years of experience working with children, adults, couples, and families. About 10 years ago we wandered, independently, into the field of separation and divorce. In addition to that of psychotherapist, we've played lots of roles, among them mediator, parenting coordinator, parenting coach, and various hybrid varieties. Although we believe passionately in our work, over time we became increasingly discouraged by the limitations of our ability to help families who had already become embedded in the family court system—itself inherently organized around the goal of identifying the "other party's" vulnerabilities and exploiting them in order to "win" a favorable outcome. By the time our clients got to us, they had usually hired attorneys and been through several rounds of nasty negotiation or, worse, litigation. They were battered and bruised, their financial and emotional resources were squandered, their mutual trust and respect were destroyed, and their children were caught in the crossfire of an ongoing battle. With rare exceptions, even though a divorcing or divorced couple might come to us hopeful that we could help them to communicate in less contentious ways and develop better co-parenting capacities, we found that so much bad blood had developed between them that their relationship was beyond repair. In many cases, we found ourselves reluctantly reduced to the role of "decision maker," a frustrating job that we are simultaneously underqualified and overqualified to perform.

Though we both practice in the Washington, D.C. Metropolitan area, we had not met until we both attended our first Collaborative Practice Training in 2006. It was a two-day introductory basic training given by Sue Brunsting of Rochester, New York. We were both immediately taken with the model, which gave us a completely new way of applying our accumulated skill and knowledge. Collaborative Practice not only offered an opportunity to get involved with a couple from the *beginning* of the divorce process (before the outside damage had been done), but also provided the framework for an integrated approach in which the needs of the family could be addressed from all directions (emotional, legal, financial). We felt we had professionally "come home" when we realized that within this model, our clients' decisions could be made out of a mutual recognition of underlying individual and family interests rather than out of fear, co-parenting relationships could be not only preserved but enhanced, and—miraculously—the children themselves could be given a voice.

Since then we have been part of the growing Collaborative Practice movement in our neck of the woods. Both of us are affiliated with several Collaborative groups, and have developed many wonderful collegial relationships (including with each other!). One of our most important shared affiliations is with The DC Academy of Collaborative Professionals (DCACP). We feel we have been collaboratively "growing up" with the other founding members of that practice group, many of whom were also at our first 2006 training. We are still in our adolescence as an organization, and we have our growing pains. But the authors are amazed at and grateful for the level of thoughtfulness, commitment, skill, and capacity for introspection in the group.

Like other Collaborative practitioners around the world, we in D.C. have grappled with the questions of "What is the right makeup of a Collaborative team?" and "Is there room for more than one type of team?" As we write, there is no consensus in the Greater Metropolitan area (D.C., Maryland, and Virginia), and the debate goes on. But, as has happened in many other Collaborative communities, we at DCACP have developed an idea of "how we do it around here." Though there have been times when we've disagreed, even heatedly, the preponderance of our membership has coalesced around the idea that in almost all cases the best Collaborative practice is a "full team approach" in which the team is composed of two attorneys, two coaches, a financial professional, and, if there are children, a child specialist. We were gratified to see that Pauline Tesler, in the second edition of her book *Collaborative Law: Achieving Effective Resolution in Divorce Without Litigation*, unambiguously put forth the full team model as being the most powerful approach for helping families as they move through this life transition.

All that said, the authors sincerely believe that not only is there room for more than one point of view, but the ongoing conversation between groups who practice in different ways lends vitality to our work. The aim of this book is not to proselytize. Rather, it is to describe the way we work, offer a theoretical framework that will apply across models, and invite dialogue about roles, team composition, and how to best serve individual clients and families.

WHY WE WROTE THIS BOOK

We have each now completed somewhere in the range of 65 Collaborative cases. We've each also had a few unsuccessful Collaborative experiences. We've learned that Collaborative doesn't mean "easy"; our work is often painfully difficult. After all, divorce, even in the rare cases in which it is a mutual decision, involves a complex set of emotions, usually including some combination of disappointment, anger, fear, shame, hurt, and grief. But beyond the obvious difficulties that accompany the task of splitting up in the face of powerful emotions, it is a psychologically complex process.

What we find is that some of our clients, even though they struggle and become positional at times in the Collaborative process, seem to respond easily and well when we help them to get in touch with the feelings behind those positions. For them, enhanced understanding in itself is sufficient to move them toward active participation. For other clients, however, we find that simply pointing out what is emotionally true is not enough. Despite our best efforts, they behave in inscrutable ways, prompting us to ask ourselves such questions as: "Why is my client making a big deal about small things?"; "Why is my client afraid of allowing her husband access to the children when he seems like a decent guy?"; "Why does my client solicit and then reject my advice?"; or "Why did these two get married in the first place?" At best, we find that our clients fluctuate, from day to day or from meeting to meeting—sometimes reasonable and open to compromise, other times rigidly inflexible. The frustration that comes with our clients behaving in stubbornly self-destructive or noncollaborative ways is an inevitable aspect of our work. And it's easy to become angry or to feel incompetent when clients seem hell-bent on shooting themselves (and us) in the foot.

> "The frustration that comes with our clients behaving in stubbornly self-destructive or noncollaborative ways is an inevitable aspect of our work."

In the introduction to their book *Collaborative Divorce: The Revolutionary Way to Restructure Your Family, Resolve Legal Issues, and Move on With Your Life*, Pauline Tesler and Peggy Thompson refer to the concept of the "shadow," an unconscious part of the self that drives human behavior. Tesler writes that "[her] attitude toward handling divorce in the courtroom changed completely when she encountered the psychologist Carl Jung's notion that every dark part of our nature that we disown, suppress, or ignore becomes part of our 'shadow' and drives our behavior in ways we don't perceive" (Tesler & Thompson, p. 6).

We appreciate the importance of Tesler and Thompson's idea that in Collaborative Practice, as in life, we all feel and act in ways that are influenced by aspects of our personalities that operate outside of our awareness. In this book, we hope to expand on that notion, further exploring the impact of unconscious emotional factors on the Collaborative process. We will look at the development of the internal worlds of our clients and ourselves, and how those worlds come alive in our work. We will examine the psychological underpinnings of the Collaborative process itself (why we do what we do), the ways in which individual professionals and their teams are affected by the emotional makeups of their clients, and the issues of assessment and technique.

Unless you are a therapist with lots of experience helping couples to separate, you might wonder why we are going to venture into what might feel like psychotherapeutic terrain. The primary answer is that unless you understand all the reasons that a couple *becomes* a couple, you can't understand what happens to them as their marriage unravels. Let's unpack that idea a bit.

We call the patterns of thinking, feeling, and behaving that characterize a particular marriage the "marital dynamics." These dynamics play out above the surface of things (in the couple's conscious awareness) and below the surface (in the couple's unconscious, out of their awareness). Think of the Collaborative team, including the clients, as a group of river rafters, and the Collaborative process as the river we navigate together.* The couple's manifest difficulties ("We would like to keep the house, but we can't afford it," or "We both want the kids for Hanukkah") are like the visible rocks that you can navigate together, if not easily, then without too much difficulty. The couple's latent troubles are like the more dangerous, invisible rocks below the surface that threaten to puncture and capsize the raft. These lurking, unseen threats are sometimes evident only as emotional white water— stubborn, baffling behaviors that cause a lot of trouble in the Collaborative process (e.g., positionality leading to impasse, provocative or abusive behavior, or threats of litigation) and that hint at larger troubles below, the location and dimensions of which we can't see. At the worst moments in our work, there isn't even the warning represented by white water. We simply find ourselves in sudden free fall—hurtled off the edge of our Collaborative river in an emotional waterfall that threatens to drown us all.

If you accept this metaphor, you can see that the successful completion of the journey to river's end—what Pauline Tesler and Peggy Thompson call a "deep peace" (Tesler & Thompson p. 162)— necessitates the development of a map for navigating a couple's

---

* The analogy between Collaborative Practice and whitewater rafting is Pauline Tesler's. She offers it, along with many other helpful metaphors, in her book Collaborative Law.

particular course, as well as tools for stabilizing the boat when the going gets rough or we wander off the map. You can also see that, in order to develop that map and those tools, we need to gather an understanding of the couple's dynamics, above and below the surface. Our book is based on the following basic assumptions:

1. The ways our clients think, feel, and behave are often driven by unconscious factors.
2. Those unconscious factors play a strong, sometimes problematic role in the course of a Collaborative case.
3. It is only by developing an understanding of the dynamics underlying our clients' patterns of thinking, feeling, and behaving that we can help them to navigate the Collaborative process.

If this sounds complicated or intimidating, don't worry. If it sounds too touchy-feely, hang in there. We are not trying to make therapists of all Collaborative practitioners. For lawyers and financial specialists, we hope to offer an introductory theoretical framework for thinking about our clients and how best to work with them. For mental health practitioners—you will already be thinking along these lines. It will be your job to apply these concepts to a formulation of your clients' individual and couple dynamics in a fuller way and, when appropriate, to share your understanding with your team in order to help move the process forward.

▼▼▼▼▼

The Conscious and the Unconscious Mind

Since the ideas in this book are predicated on a recognition and understanding of the concepts of a conscious and unconscious mind, it makes sense to offer quick definitions:

The Conscious Mind

Our conscious mind is composed of all the memories, ideas, thoughts, and feelings of which we are aware. Even though, at any given moment, we can only be actively thinking about a small portion of our consciousness, its contents are accessible to us—we can easily recall any aspect of it at will.

The Unconscious Mind

We're consciously aware of a small part of what's going on in our minds. The part of us driving the way we think, feel, and behave that's operating outside of our conscious awareness we call the unconscious. Our unconscious wields a lot of power over us. If you've ever had a disturbing dream that brought to the surface of your thoughts something you hadn't been thinking about before, if you've ever made a "Freudian slip," or "accidentally" forgotten a meeting that deep-down you wanted to avoid, then you've seen the evidence.

A note on our source material and our decision not to footnote specific psychological concepts: Many of the ideas upon which we draw in this book form the very fabric of psychodynamic theory. They are like air and water to clinicians—ubiquitous to the point that citing a particular theorist is difficult. Still, we can trace many ideas fairly close to their sources. The concept of a "conscious" and "unconscious" mind as well as initial ideas about "transference" and "countertransference" originated with Sigmund Freud. Later, he and his daughter Anna Freud began the discussion of ego defenses that are now part of common parlance. The ideas in Section I are an extraction, synthesis, and new application of ideas that come from Object Relations theory, a theory of human development based on the idea that the dominant determinant of personality formation is our experience in relationships. The chapters on individual dynamics, couple dynamics, and the collaborative container rely heavily on the writings of Donald Winnicott (who richly described the way in which the safe psychological space—or "holding environment"—created by the mother is what allows the baby to find its self), the work of Wilfred Bion (who introduced the term "containment" to explain the internal process by which the mother—and later the baby—takes in and processes anxiety), Melanie Klein's (and later others') description of the process of "projective identification," W.R.D. Fairbairn's model of endopsychic organization, and David and Jill Scharff's (and others') synthesis of Object Relations and group relations theory into a model for understanding couple formation and family functioning. The concepts of the Lock and Key, the two-part Collaborative container, and the Rigidity/Flexibility Continuum are the authors', but readers who choose to explore psychoanalytic theory in general (and Object Relations theory in specific) will soon recognize the origins of our ideas (see "References" section for relevant source material).

Understanding Our Clients and Ourselves

INDIVIDUAL DYNAMICS

1

PORTRAITS OF TWO
COLLABORATIVE CLIENTS*

Dan *came to the Collaborative process traumatized and reeling. Laura, his wife of 15 years, had recently and suddenly announced that she was in love with her employer, Bill. To make matters worse, she admitted she had been secretly channeling marital funds into her lover's start-up business. Dan was understandably furious and devastated. He initially consulted a "gladiator" attorney, who told him that he would likely "win" primary custody and financial restitution if he pursued the matter in court. Still, Dan's greatest concern was the impact of his wife's behavior on his children. Although his trust in Laura had been shaken to the core, Dan was somehow able to hold in mind the fact that he would have to co-parent with her forever. He decided to hire a Collaborative attorney.*

---

*These are two separate clients, not a divorcing couple.

Dan required extensive emotional support during the Collaborative process. While he understood his children's need for equal time with their mother, he sometimes felt she should be punished for her "amoral" behavior. Most painfully, he struggled with the knowledge that his children would eventually be spending time with the man with whom Laura had betrayed him. Even so, Dan was able to make use of his attorney and coach in keeping his children's needs foremost in his mind. Although he was in terrible emotional pain, Dan had faith in the team. In turn, the team was able to work with the couple to craft an agreement based not on a desire for retribution but on the many needs of the entire family.

__Tiffany__ was skeptical and only tentatively engaged in the Collaborative process from the beginning. She declined to hire the first Collaborative attorney she interviewed (an experienced and widely respected practitioner) because, Tiffany claimed, the attorney was not sufficiently "interested and caring." Tiffany's evidence for this was that the attorney "took a telephone call from another client" during their first interview. In fact, the attorney's receptionist had mistakenly put a call through during the meeting, but the attorney had quickly hung up and apologized to Tiffany for the interruption.

Tiffany painted a picture of her marriage as one in which she was mentally abused, and of her husband, Joe, as an uncaring philanderer who had abandoned her and was out to "screw her" financially. In fact, while the marriage had been a tumultuous one, it was Tiffany herself who had had multiple affairs. Her husband had made the final decision to end the marriage, but only after years of threats by Tiffany and several unsuccessful rounds of marital counseling.

There were few marital assets, but Joe had brought to the marriage considerable wealth and stood to inherit a great deal more. While he did begin a new relationship soon after their separation, he consistently voiced a desire to ensure financial security for Tiffany and their twin daughters. Despite his understanding that he would likely "win" the right to keep the bulk of his money if he were to pursue traditional negotiation, Joe willingly entered the Collaborative process.

During meetings Tiffany's demeanor ranged from hypersensitive to enraged. She monopolized the discussion, insisting that team members did not understand the ways in which Joe intimidated and abused her. She accused the team of being "on Joe's side," and complained that her needs were being ignored. She frequently telephoned her attorney, coach, and financial neutral (often in the evenings and on the weekends), and became furious when she did not receive an immediate response. When any member of the team attempted to reassure her of their concern for her and their commitment to making sure the process would be fair and open, she would calm down for a time. But she would rev up again whenever she sensed any movement in the team toward compromise and away from her polarized position.

For now, we invite you to simply hold these portraits in your mind as we talk a bit about how individuals develop some of their strengths and vulnerabilities—in other words, how a Dan becomes a Dan and a Tiffany becomes a Tiffany.

THE INFLUENCE OF EARLY EXPERIENCE

We are all born into relationships. We interact first with our closest caregivers (usually our parents), other immediate family members, and babysitters. Then our circles widen to include extended family, friends, authority figures, institutions, and cultures. While the quality of our experience in relationships (and thus our modes of relating) can and does change over the course of our lives, it is our earliest relationships that exert the most influence over how we relate to ourselves and others. When we are young, we absorb the ways that our important people think, feel, and behave—with us and with each other. We take our observations and experiences inside ourselves, where they form the core of our growing identities.

How does this happen? As an example, let's think of a typical daily interaction between a newborn and his mother. The baby has no awareness of where he ends and his mother begins. The baby is a stranger to his mother, yet completely dependent on her. They are getting to know each other. So when the baby cries the mother becomes concerned; she wants to make sense of her baby's distress. In this scenario let's imagine the mother is emotionally healthy. She rocks her baby, her whole self (body and mind) attuned to him, trying to make sense of his communication. "Are you hungry?" she coos. But she offers the breast and the baby turns away. "Maybe you're wet," she says. Gently, she lays the baby down and changes him. The baby relaxes, his discomfort relieved. "Ah, that's it," she sighs, and the baby allows her to lay him in his bassinet for a nap.

In this simple set of interactions, many important things have happened. The baby has had an overwhelming experience. The mother has registered it and, because she is a loving parent, has become somewhat anxious. But she has not become overwhelmed by her anxiety. She has maintained a calm, loving stance toward the baby, offering one possible solution, then another. Once she has reflected on and found the root of the baby's discomfort, the baby is soothed and the mother relieved and proud. Though he doesn't know it, the baby has been given the message that pain, physical and emotional, can be borne and thought about without causing damage. Over time and thousands of such interactions, the baby will internalize not only a trust in those around him but a trust in his own capacity to bear frustration and distress and to make meaning out of them. This feeling of basic trust in others, as well as in one's own capacity to tolerate, reflect on, and make sense of experience, builds self-esteem and is essential to a child's growing capacity to form loving relationships.

> "... basic trust in others, as well as in one's own capacity to tolerate, reflect on, and make sense of experience, builds self-esteem and is essential to the child's growing capacity to form loving relationships."

Now, let's consider a baby born with a similar disposition, but with a less emotionally healthy mother. The baby cries, and the mother tenses. "What's wrong?" she asks, her anxiety evident in her voice and body language. She offers the baby her breast, and, when the baby turns away, she tries to push her nipple into the baby's mouth. When that doesn't work, the mother's anxiety mounts. She paces nervously, bouncing the baby and attempting awkwardly to soothe her. The baby's cries grow louder and both baby and mother feel more tension and urgency. By the time the mother finally changes the baby's diaper, the baby's distress has risen to a point where she is difficult to soothe and the mother feels frustrated, inept, and perhaps even angry at the baby and at herself. Over years and thousands of such interactions, this baby internalizes a quite different set of messages than the baby described previously. For this baby, painful thoughts and feelings will represent intolerable states that cannot be thought about or named, let alone borne, understood, and satisfied. This baby may develop a sense of herself as greedy and insatiable, and a belief that her own needs are unacceptable and capable of causing damage. The baby with an inadequate mother will fail to develop a sense of basic trust in others; her self-esteem, her capacity for self-reflection, and her capacity to form loving relationships will be compromised.

In ensuing years, the implications of these early experiences will have a cascading effect. The sense of well-being and trust that the first baby experienced in his early relationships will be carried over into subsequent ones. His childhood experience of the world as a safe place where his needs are reflected on, understood, and met, and his experience of his own mind as one that can tolerate, make sense of, and find ways to satisfy itself, will allow him to go on to form other positive relationships. Other people with whom he comes in contact will see him as someone who offers and expects a satisfactory mutuality in relating, and they will be likely to respond in kind. Even when he experiences loss and betrayal, he will be able to call on his own internal resources to get him through.

Now think of Dan: in the face of betrayal by his wife he felt the normal, expectable range of emotions—anger, sadness, fear, even the passing desire for retribution. Still, overall, he was able to hold on to the idea that his wife was not *all* bad—his children needed her in the way they needed him. His lack of trust in his wife did not shake his trust in the Collaborative team. He was able to lean on team members to support him in weathering the vicissitudes of his own emotions and to aid him in accessing his better nature. The result was that he was able to behave in ways consistent with his core values.

On the other hand, the baby with the inadequate mother in the latter example is likely to enter new situations from a place of paranoia. Her early experiences will drive her to meet new people with anxiety and mistrust, and new people will respond to these expectations in such a way that she is likely to get what she expects. Now consider Tiffany. To her, every situation and every new person represented a threat. While her husband and her Collaborative team were steadfastly committed to supporting her in getting a fair outcome, she remained distrustful, angry, and dissatisfied. While she was able to emerge from the process with a favorable Agreement, she remained stuck in a position of entitled rage, forever pursuing an unattainable retribution that she was convinced would eventually satisfy her need for justice.

So does this mean that unless we are fortunate enough to have a mother as easily responsive to our needs as the mother in the first example, we are doomed to be a "Tiffany," ever angry, pushing away those who might otherwise care about us? No. The good news is that we internalize not one pattern of relating, but several. All parents have strengths *and* vulnerabilities. The anxious mother who has difficulty coping with her baby's distress might also be an energetic, expressive person who cultivates in her child a sense of wonder and creativity. Also, all of us have early relationships with not one, but several important figures. The effects of difficult interactions with one person can be mitigated by positive interactions with others. Even the baby in the second example, the one with the anxious mother, can become more trusting, and therefore more capable of meeting new experiences with optimism. Say, for example, she has a father who can more easily bear and respond to her needs. The baby will internalize aspects of this more positive relationship as well.

And even though our earliest relationships are the most formative, our development is ongoing (and therapists and Collaborative practitioners count on that idea!). Let's say our troubled baby has a wonderful kindergarten teacher who is able to identify her difficulties, talk about them, and offer support and new ways of relating. What if, for example, the teacher repeatedly says things like, "Tiffany, I know you're worried that the other children are going to make fun of you when you have trouble saying good-bye to your mommy. Lots of children miss their parents. Why don't you sit with me for a while and listen to a story, then, when you're ready, you can join the others who are building with blocks?" Here the teacher will have done what Tiffany's mother failed to do. She will have identified the child's discomfort and named the resultant anxiety without rushing in too quickly to alleviate it, communicated her faith in little Tiffany's ability to manage her feelings, normalized her experience, and offered strategies for coping. Tiffany's mother will continue to behave in familiar ways, but over time those ways may affect Tiffany less intensely. She will internalize the new and better experiences she has with her empathic teacher, and will begin to develop an improved sense of herself and the world. Newly satisfying experiences will beget more of the same, thus creating a feedback loop with the power to modify, or at least to mitigate, Tiffany's established negative patterns of relating. The resultant strengthened sense of self-esteem may also mean that Tiffany is less susceptible to feeling bad or falling into old behaviors when she relates to her mother or to someone who reminds her of her mother.

In the case of little Tiffany, negative experience is modified by good when the kindergarten teacher steps in. Unfortunately, it can also work the other way. We already talked about how the lucky baby in our first example would likely grow into a constitutionally optimistic adult. But let's say this baby experiences a traumatic event during toddlerhood, childhood, adolescence, or even adulthood. Say he suffers a serious injury, loses a loved one, or is physically or sexually assaulted. Even ordinary reasoning tells us that his sense of the world as a safe place, of other people and himself as reliable, and his openness to new relationships will be negatively impacted. The question is, in what ways and to what extent? The answer to that question is essential for us to think about because it offers us some important ways of understanding our Collaborative clients and how to work with them most effectively.

THE SHOWDOWN BETWEEN GOOD AND BAD EXPERIENCE

Since all of our lives are made up of good and bad experiences, how is it that some of us grow up to be fundamentally happy and successful while others of us become fundamentally unhappy and unsuccessful? What determines which experiences (and which people in our lives) are going to exert the most influence?

We all know people who have lived privileged lives and still manage to be miserable. They grew up loved and supported but not overindulged, were afforded great educational opportunities, and never suffered significant trauma. Still, they are professional underachievers, don't have satisfactory personal lives, or simply find baseless reasons to complain. We all also know people who seem to defy reasoning in the opposite way. They grow up in atmospheres of emotional and financial deprivation, suffer terrible trauma, yet they succeed professionally and personally and seem eternally optimistic. Some people seem hardwired for unhappiness and failure, while others seem to flourish even under the harshest circumstances. It's the old nature versus nurture puzzle. Why do some people make excuses while others make hay?

The truth is that people who defy the odds are rare. Most people display attitudes and behaviors that follow logically from their early lives. Important personality traits—the capacity or incapacity to form loving relationships or to find and maintain satisfying work—can be directly linked to formative experiences. To some extent, there is a simple mathematical way of thinking about this: the more our early experience is good the happier we will be and vice versa.

But this simplistic formula breaks down when we consider that personality is neither linear nor static. We are not simply happy or not, successful or not. We are three-dimensional dynamic beings. So, for example, a person with a domineering, critical father may struggle professionally because of conflict with authority figures. At the same time, this person may have had a nurturing mother and may enjoy success as a confident, successful parent. Also, as we've already described, our personalities evolve over time. Even though our childhood experiences exert the most powerful influence over us, even entrenched thoughts, feelings, and ways of relating can be modified by powerful new experiences (including a good Collaborative divorce).

It turns out that bad experiences, whether ongoing (such as being raised by the critical father in the above example or suffering from a chronic debilitating illness) or represented by a single traumatic event (such as the death of a loved one), exert more influence over the formation of our characters than positive ones. The worse an experience, the more influential. Why? Because it takes more emotional energy, more of our *selves*, to manage the feelings associated with bad experiences than good ones. We'll explain.

EMOTIONAL DEFENSES

All of us protect ourselves against (in other words, manage to go on *in spite of*) negative or traumatic experiences through various unconscious psychological strategies known in the mental health field as "defenses." We might push feelings or memories out of our awareness ("repression"), insist to ourselves and to others that our feelings are mild when they are actually intense ("minimization"), deny that an event affected us or even occurred ("denial"), or distract ourselves from an emotional situation by focusing on other issues or tasks ("avoidance"). There are other emotional defenses we could describe, and we'll get to some of them later. But we hope we've given you enough of the flavor of the phenomena that we can turn our attention to the larger impact of defenses on us and our clients.

THE IMPACT OF DEFENSES ON OUR CAPACITY TO FUNCTION

Defenses are not always problematic; in fact, we couldn't make it through a day without them. We couldn't be productive workers (or parents or spouses) if we were steadily preoccupied with global crises or the ordinary dangers of everyday life. It is the extent of our reliance on defenses—how often we move into protective mode, how long we linger there, and how entrenched our defensive postures become—that shape the way we cope, both in our ordinary lives and during times of stress (such as divorce).

Here's why: Think of your emotional energy as money in your psychic bank. You have a finite amount. Choosing *not* to think about or remember something (to defend against it) doesn't come free; in fact, it's very costly. Once you force a painful memory out of your conscious awareness, it's not really buried. It's just exiled to your unconscious, where it lurks and threatens to break back through. You will have to continue to spend emotional money in order to keep it there. Defenses are mentally expensive; trying to feel less or not feel at all costs a lot of emotional currency. That's currency that is then not available to spend on other, more productive pursuits, such as the two pillars of a productive life—work and love.

> "Think of your emotional energy as money in your psychic bank. You have a finite amount. Choosing not to think about or remember something (to defend against it) doesn't come free; in fact, it's very costly."

So when a client behaves in perplexing or provocative ways, ask yourself, "Is this someone whose defenses are getting in the way of effective functioning?" For example, consider a client who appears upset at the end of a meeting but insists that he is "fine," only to send an enraged e-mail to his spouse that evening. This client is likely utilizing the defense of denial to protect him from uncomfortable feelings at the meeting, and experiencing a later breakdown of his defense. Take another client who repeatedly forgets to complete homework assignments in preparation for financial meetings. This client may be employing avoidance as protection from her anxiety about finances. Similarly, parents who smile through the first coaching four-way meeting and assure you and each other that they "agree about everything and should be able to get through this in an hour or so" might be a fabulously healthy and cooperative pair, *or* they might share the emotional defenses of denial and minimization. As we explained in the Introduction, the point here is not to turn all Collaborative practitioners into therapists who can expertly and confidently analyze their

> "If you can stay tuned in to the existence of these latent feelings (the rocks that lurk beneath the surface of the Collaborative river) and try to make sense of them, you will have taken the first step in learning to help your clients more efficiently, compassionately, and productively."

clients. Rather, we want to stress the importance of remembering that difficult behaviors in our clients often reflect attempts to stave off painful states of mind. If you can stay tuned in to the existence of these *latent* feelings (the rocks that lurk beneath the surface of the Collaborative river) and try to make sense of them, you will have taken the first step in learning to help your clients more efficiently, compassionately, and productively.

▼▼▼▼▼
Examples of the Healthy Use of Defenses

Sally's mother dies. Friends comment that she seems eerily cheerful and disconnected from her grief. On the other hand, Sally is able to complete a complicated legal brief at work, a task on which her job depends. With the task completed, Sally no longer needs to repress her feelings about her mother's death. During the months that follow, she is able to face and work through her grief.

Steven's only son, Mark, is deployed to a combat unit in Iraq. Steven daily reassures his wife and his two other children that Mark's training and competence will keep him out of harm's way. Only when Mark returns safely many months later is his father able to relinquish his denial and feel the full impact of the anxiety he had been carrying.

MENTAL HEALTH AND ILL-HEALTH

Mental health can be measured, in large part, by an individual's capacity to relate to a range of people and situations in a range of ways. The broader the range, the healthier the person. A healthy individual is capable of seeing the world in shades of gray, capable of seeing him- or herself in a realistically nuanced way, capable of recognizing others' points of view, and perhaps most importantly

> ▼
> "Mental health can be measured, in large part, by an individual's capacity to perceive and relate to a range of people and situations in a range of ways. The broader the range, the healthier the person."

for our work, capable of ownership of his or her own feelings and behaviors and of course correction.

Think of a colleague who seems to meet every new situation in the same way. Say, for example, he seems always to feel that people are ready to exploit or take advantage of him, even when there is no evidence to support that idea. Or think of a friend who seems always to experience you as disinterested or not listening, when, in fact, you are exhausted from her constant need for a sympathetic ear. What's going on?

Highly traumatized individuals behave in stereotypical ways. Why? Because the fact that they have to work so hard to keep painful thoughts and feelings outside of their conscious awareness means that there is not much of their psychic energy (their "selves") left over for spontaneous, realistic relating in the here and now. They must resort to living according to a set of preset templates, modes of relating that are narrow in scope and number. They become caricatures.

Of course none of us escapes trauma. Each of us has both good and bad experiences. To some extent, we have all repressed, minimized, or otherwise defended against painful memories and the feelings and ideas associated with them. In other words, we all have characterological vulnerabilities, pesky hot spots in our personalities that cause us to behave in predictably difficult ways and compromise our abilities to see the world as it is.

For example, if, as a child, you felt you could do no right in your mother's eyes, you might, as an adult, be hypersensitive to feed-

> ▼
> "We all have characterological vulnerabilities, pesky hot spots in our personalities that cause us to behave in predictably difficult ways and compromise our abilities to see the world as it is."

back from others, even when it is well-intended or potentially helpful. Similarly, if one of your parents was unfaithful to the other during your childhood, you might find that you too quickly judge clients who stray, rather than holding back until you can see the behavior in its full context within their marriage.

As Collaborative practitioners, the question we should ask ourselves is not *whether or not* our clients sometimes adopt irrational positions, develop distorted ideas, or overreact. They are human, and they will. The important questions are *How often will they do these things? Under what conditions?* and *Are they capable of recovery when they do?* In other words, how much emotional energy is available in their psychic banks? How much flexibility do they have in the ways they meet and relate to the world, to others in it, and, most importantly for us, to each other? Are they restricted to one rigid template, or do they have a wide range of feeling, being, and perceiving?

REVIEW

In this chapter, we took a close look at how our earliest relationships form the core of our characters. We explored the formative power of positive and negative experiences. We discussed emotional defenses, and the ways they can distort our view of the world. Finally, we linked the concepts of mental health and ill-health to an individual's range of modes of relating to others. Now that we've looked at the development of an individual personality, let's turn our attention to the development of a couple's personality.

COUPLE DYNAMICS 2

HOW COUPLES COME TOGETHER
AND HOW THEY COME APART

A couple is more than the sum of its parts. The complicated emotional makeup of one person comes together with that of the other, they become intertwined in a myriad of ways and—voila—a third entity is formed, a partnership comprised of the qualities of each, but having its own new characteristics. That's why good couples therapists know that their client is not the individuals in the room, but the couple itself. They know, too, that in order to understand a couple you must understand the individual members of the couple, what draws each to the other, and what psychological alchemical reaction occurred when their personalities were joined.

Think about a number of couples you know well—clients you work with, your sister and brother-in-law, your best friends, your parents, you and your partner. Think about how those couples "fit" together in some obvious ways, some of which may be charming and amusing and some of which may set your teeth on edge.

As an example, let's look at a newly wed couple we'll call Miranda and Bob. Bob is a CPA who likes to be prompt, keeps his side of the closet organized to a T, and provides Miranda with a reliability and predictability she yearned for after growing up in an alcoholic family. Miranda is an art therapist who runs late, drops her dirty clothes on the floor despite Bob's constant nagging, and provides Bob with laughter, spontaneity, and a whimsical love of adventure that he sorely lacked in the lonely and professorial home in which he grew up. If you know Bob and Miranda, you know that Bob helps Miranda get places on time, and Miranda makes the dinner conversation livelier while Bob helps with the dishes. They each seem to enjoy the aspects of the other's personality that they lack in their own.

Now, we'll look at Miranda and Bob ten years into their marriage. Bob is continually annoyed with Miranda for making him late and being disorganized. Miranda is fed up with Bob's constricted rules of living, and both find the other intensely irritating and tiresome. Bob has grown to see Miranda's creative spontaneity as a willful refusal to plan in thoughtful ways, and Miranda has grown to see Bob's reliability and predictability as boring, stultifying, and a purposeful insistence on squeezing the life out of their marriage. Both Bob and Miranda wonder why they ever got married. How do we understand this shift?

PROJECTION AND THE "LOCK AND KEY" CONCEPT

All romantic couples are brought together by a combination of factors. Some they can easily recognize, such as shared values and physical attraction. These are what we might refer to as "conscious" factors. Others, of which potential partners might not be aware, we might refer to as "unconscious" factors. These unconscious factors exist and exert influence beneath the surface of awareness. As we discussed in the previous chapter, unconscious aspects of our characters represent old conflicts that we have not fully faced and worked through, and that are too painful or uncomfortable for our conscious selves to face. We already talked about some of the defenses that we use to keep these unconscious ideas out of our consciousness—repression, denial, minimization, and avoidance. Another common defense is projection.

The concept of projection is particularly important for us to think about here because it plays a powerful unconscious role in the formation of a couple. In the last chapter, we talked about the way we take in (or *internalize*) experience, both good and bad; it becomes a part of us. Through the mechanism of projection, a part of the self, a characteristic, is split off from our conscious sense of our self and projected *out* and *into* another. Sometimes what is projected out is a hated aspect of our self; sometimes it is a treasured part of our self that cannot find safe expression.

Let's look at a couple of examples. Say you were abused as a child. Because you were a child you needed to preserve the idea that the adults around you were good, competent people on whom you could rely. The only way you had to maintain that view, and to regain a sense of control in an out-of-control situation, was to develop the idea that you were responsible for the abuse. That is why abuse is particularly toxic—it affects the way we feel not only about the abuser but, more importantly, about ourselves. You might come to think of yourself as someone worthy of abuse, or as someone capable of abuse, or both. These bad feelings about yourself would cause you discomfort, would threaten your self-esteem. You would want to be rid of them. Through the process of projection, you could free yourself of these negative ideas about yourself through your choice of a partner in whom you could project those aspects of yourself that caused you pain. For example, you could choose an abusive partner. That would allow you to say to yourself,

> "... while projection works to defend against psychic pain on a conscious level, it also gets us into trouble in relationships."

"He is the abusive one; I am not." You could also say to yourself, "See, he thinks I am worthy of abuse." Unfortunately, while projection works to defend against psychic pain on a conscious level, it also gets us into trouble in relationships. You can see that, in this example, even though you've managed to rid yourself of the conscious idea of yourself as worthy or capable of abuse, you've picked an abusive partner. Your relationship will be difficult and, in the end, reinforce the negative ideas you had about yourself from the start.

Here's another example. Let's say you were a highly creative child raised in a restrictive environment in which creative expression was frowned upon. You might choose a partner who is a wonderful dancer and painter, and take great pleasure in his or her expressivity. Other times, you might be irritated or jealous. Either way, here would not be a hated part of you being projected into the other, but a beloved part. Located in your partner, it could be kept safe from imagined emotional attack.

From the above examples, you can see that projection serves both adaptive and maladaptive functions. It protects us from uncomfortable feelings such as shame and anger and, as in the latter example, allows us to take pleasure in areas of our lives that might not be available to us otherwise. On the other hand, it can cause difficulty. As in all other defensive mechanisms, projection is unconscious. Just as repression doesn't do away with unwanted ideas, feelings, or memories (it simply exiles them to the unconscious where they continue to exert influence), projection doesn't really do away with the part of ourselves that we want to be rid of. When what is projected is related to trauma (as in the first example), acrimonious relationships are formed. When what is projected is a beloved but threatened part of the self (as in the second example), a fragile peace is formed.

By way of illustration, let's refer back to Bob and Miranda. With the concept of projection in mind, we can see that Bob has projected the spontaneous, creative parts of himself into Miranda. For her part, Miranda has projected her own needs for structure, safety, and predictability into Bob. Their marriage went well to the extent that their defenses held up and they were able to take pleasure in their complementarity. But over time, their defenses broke down (perhaps due to characterological changes in one of them, or perhaps due to environmental changes or stresses, such as the birth of a child or a financial reversal). At that point, the cherished differences between them became points of contention.

You may very well ask yourself, "Why are the authors singling projection out from the other defenses as being particularly important for couples?" What makes projection special and critical to understanding how couples fit together is that, unlike other defenses, projection is a mutual process. In order to be activated as a force in bringing members of a couple together or driving their attitudes and behavior toward each other, it must have the cooperation of two people—someone to project and another to receive.

Miranda could not feel entitled to treat Bob as a substitute parent if he didn't allow her to, and Bob could not rely on Miranda to enliven his life if she were not up to the task. Unconsciously, we all seek to find a partner who is willing, also unconsciously, to be the recipient of our projections. And we, in turn and also unconsciously, must be willing to accept theirs. This process of mutual projection and the qualities of the resultant relationship are what the authors come to think of as the "Lock and Key": the unique way in which a couple comes together—their unique "fit."

> "... unlike other defenses, projection is a mutual process ... it must have the cooperation of two people—someone to project and another to receive. ... Unconsciously, we all seek to find a partner who is willing ... to be the recipient of our projections. And we, in turn ... must be willing to accept theirs."

In the last chapter, we discussed the fact that there is a direct relationship between the amounts of early trauma we experience and the need for defenses against the memories and feelings associated with that trauma. We explained that the more energy we must spend on emotional defenses, the less energy is left over to us to relate freely—to our self and to others. What is true for the other defenses is true for projection. The more we need to use projection in order to feel okay about ourselves, the more projection drives the way we relate to others—especially to those we are closest to.

To the extent that projection is a feature of a romantic relationship, the more likely it is that the individuals in a couple will see each other in distorted, exaggerated, polarized, or caricatured ways. In other words, heavy use of projection by two partners will cause them to relate to each other in stereotypical ways based on their individual histories, rather than in flexible ways based

▼

"In the same way that individual health can be measured by the ability to relate to people and situations in a variety of ways, the health of a couple can be measured by the capacity of its members to relate to each other in a variety of realistic ways."

on a realistic understanding of each other's subjective feelings and perspectives. The more projection is at work in the formation of the couple, the more rigidity, fragility, and brittleness is in the relationship. In the same way that individual health can be measured by the ability to relate to people and situations in a variety of ways, the health of a couple can be measured by the capacity of its members to relate to each other in a variety of realistic ways.

It is critical to keep in mind that projection is a two-way street that serves an important function for both members of the couple. Projection protects the couple by creating an emotional homeostasis for both. Dysfunctional as a marital dynamic may appear to us, it serves to provide psychic equilibrium for both. So when a couple divorces, when they lose the ability to rely on each other as the recipient of important projections, they lose the ability to defend against uncomfortable feelings about themselves. The result is what we see when we interview people in the first stages of separation and divorce: destabilization, fear, cognitive impairment, depression, anxiety—the gamut of emotions that come when our psychological world is rent asunder.

It is worth noting that repression and the other defense mechanisms we've discussed also play an important role in bringing people together in relationships. After all, when we form what we hope will be a lifelong partnership, we are choosing to spend the rest of our lives with another person who is inevitably flawed. And we don't have the biological imperative of a blood relationship to protect us. The only way we can manage this is by repressing, minimizing, or denying some of our awareness of our partner's flaws, or at least our awareness of how much these flaws do or could bother us. After all, what is romantic love but the elevation of certain qualities of the other and the soft-pedaling of others? We say to ourselves, "He's a little loose with money, but I love his generosity," or "She's always on my heels cleaning up, but she keeps me in line." Once we have committed to each other, if things go well, the idealization remains in place long enough for the growth of the lasting mutual indulgence that comes with the development of a shared history.

One of the most painful aspects of divorce is that in order to face the overwhelming feelings associated with deciding to terminate a once loving relationship, we must denigrate the qualities in the other that we once idealized. So, "He's a little loose with money, but I love his generosity" becomes "He's spending us into the ground." "She's always on my heels cleaning up, but she keeps me in line" becomes "She's an unbearable harpy." This repudiation of once-beloved qualities can be particularly painful for a spouse who does not want the divorce or is not as far along in the grieving process as the other. For them, the devaluing by their spouse of once-valued character traits can feel like an unbearable betrayal.

> "... in order to face the overwhelming feelings associated with deciding to terminate a once loving relationship, we must denigrate the qualities in the other that we once idealized."

Let's highlight a few important points we've covered so far:

1. Projection is a mutual defense mechanism that, while potentially problematic, maintains psychic homeostasis for the individual and for the couple.
2. Depending on the extent of the use of projection by the couple, it will play a relatively large or small role in the way they relate to each other.
3. The health of the couple can be measured by the capacity of each person to see the other as he or she really is, rather than as the person imagines him or her to be.
4. Repression plays a role, along with projection, as an important unconscious factor drawing spouses together.
5. When a couple splits (when a Lock loses its Key and vice versa), they lose important defensive mechanisms and become highly emotionally destabilized.

6. When a couple splits, they must denigrate in each other that which they once idealized. This fact can often be experienced by one or both members of the couple as an unimaginable betrayal.

ISABEL AND ALAN: PORTRAIT OF A DIVORCING COUPLE

Alan grew up the only child of two serious and socially isolated parents in a quiet Midwestern suburb. As a child, he was loved and cared for, bright and athletic. Still, he felt lonely and shy—on the social periphery. Alan did not date or become sexually active until he was a junior in college, a fact he found privately humiliating. He described himself as always having been cautious and anxious, ever vigilant for what "might go wrong" (a trait he inherited from his mother). Still, he felt frustrated with his own inhibition, and yearned to be more of a risk-taker—able to grab for the brass ring.

By contrast, Isabel grew up in a large boisterous family in an urban Italian-American neighborhood. She also was loved and cared for, but had to work hard for attention from her busy parents, who were often preoccupied with her siblings and large extended family. Isabel's parents struggled financially, and Isabel resented having to work for her own spending money. She was an outgoing girl, hungry for attention and happy in the spotlight. She generally chose short-term pleasure over long-term gain.

The two met when Alan was a supervisor in the same small company where Isabel first worked after college. Although he was only two years her senior, Alan seemed to Isabel like a "grown-up man." She felt girlish and irresponsible, still wanting to have fun and avoid adult concerns. Alan represented stability; he seemed to her someone who would work hard, succeed, and provide well. Isabel found Alan's quiet personality compelling, though she particularly appreciated his enjoyment of the funny, entertaining aspects of her own character. She was both intimidated and impressed by his parents, whom she experienced as cultured and elegant. The quiet of Alan's tree-lined childhood neighborhood represented fulfillment of a fantasy of a lovely, clean, easy life, free of physically tiring, boring work.

When Alan met Isabel, he fell hard. He was drawn to her showy attractiveness, lively personality, and popularity. Her talkativeness put him at ease; he was comfortable in the role of appreciative listener. He could feel her admiration for his intelligence, maturity, and ability to provide for her then and in the future. When Alan saw himself in Isabel's eyes, he felt less lonely and more potent. When he met and was embraced by Isabel's gregarious and happy family, his fate was sealed. The two became engaged after only four months.

Seven years later, Alan and Isabel were the parents of two girls, ages five and three. They lived in a close-in suburb of the city where Isabel grew up. Alan, who had been promoted, worked long hours. Though concerned about the family income, Alan had capitulated to Isabel's desire to stay home with the children rather than going out to work. Over the years, though, her tendency to overspend had landed the couple in debt. This caused Alan considerable anxiety, and drove him to work even harder. The couple fell into a pattern in which Isabel felt increasingly neglected by Alan, and he felt increasingly overwhelmed and burdened by a sense of disappointing his wife.

What Alan once loved in his wife—her lively, carefree spirit—he now saw as irresponsible indifference to the realities of their situation. He began to yearn for the kind of concerned, focused attention he had received from his mother. Alan felt himself pulling away from Isabel, feeling judgmental about her spending habits, and newly impatient with the extended family activities that seemed to fill every weekend.

Isabel began to spend increasing periods of time in the city with friends, sometimes staying away from the family overnight. She reconnected with Jake, an old flame, in whom she refound an appreciative, attentive partner who helped her to feel young, free, and unencumbered.

Eventually, Alan discovered a long history of sexualized e-mail exchanges between Isabel and Jake. When confronted, Isabel became tearfully apologetic, but announced plans to move to the city and to continue to see Jake (whom, unbeknownst to Alan, she had already introduced to their children on several occasions).

The couple, having resolved to terminate their marriage, made their way into the Collaborative process. Alan alternated between resignation about the divorce and a desire for reconciliation. At times, he admitted that he had been angry at and disdainful of his wife for some time. He recognized that he had indulged Isabel "like a child," not insisting that she "face reality" by curbing her spending and working with him on their growing emotional distance. In other moments, Alan seethed in quiet rage, seeing Isabel as a gold digger and himself as an innocent victim.

Isabel was able to admit some sadness about the end of the marriage and, when pushed, acknowledged some shame at her selfish choices. But she quickly moved away from these more uncomfortable feelings to a minimization of her losses and the impact of the divorce on her husband and children. She said, "These things happen, and it will all work out in the end." She also assumed the children would live full-time with her (and, eventually, Jake). Alan, when faced with this assumption, felt duped and furious. He accused her of trying to replace him with Jake, an idea he found unbearable.

ISABEL AND ALAN'S LOCK AND KEY

Isabel and Alan, when asked what originally drew them together, were each easily able to recall the aspects of the other's personality and background they had found compelling. What they were unable to recognize or articulate was the way they had sought and found in each other recompense for early pain and loss and a completion of "holes" in their own characters. In Alan, Isabel had found the status and stability she had not felt as a child. She also found support for her desire to avoid adult responsibility, a fear grounded in her relationship to her own parents. In Isabel, Alan found the exciting, sexual, social aspects of himself that had been missing, and relief from a sense of himself as damaged and unappealing. Isabel's admiration of him and reliance on him stood in stark contrast to his mother's smothering anxiety. Eventually, though, as happens with so many couples, Isabel and Alan found each other lacking. After all, neither of them really had the power to make up for what the other had suffered as a child. During the early years of their marriage, both spouses saw in each other what they wanted to see. As time passed, and children, laundry, and bills were added to the mix, both Alan and Isabel fell off the pedestal. Alan became weary of Isabel's childlike selfishness. When he felt impatient with her, she felt his criticism and missed his admiration. When Alan's desire for her waned, due to work fatigue, parenting fatigue, and his growing irritation with her, Isabel no longer felt she got the attention she deserved and so sorely needed. This made her seek attention elsewhere. She became more apt to see Alan's faults. Their inability to negotiate the complicated psychic dance in which they were engaged resulted, ultimately, in the failure of their marriage.

THE LOCK AND KEY MANIFESTED IN THE COLLABORATIVE PROCESS

As we've discussed, the divorcing couples that we see as Collaborative practitioners are often stuck in old modes of relating that include projection as a primary defense mechanism. Alan had projected his own social and sexual strivings and desire to be free of care and responsibility into Isabel, but in time he came to resent those same traits. Isabel projected into Alan her desire for stability, status, and safety, traits by which she came to feel persecuted. While the marriage worked, Alan and Isabel were each able to establish and maintain their individual psychic stability through their unconscious reliance on each other. But the loss of each other destabilized each of them in ways that were subsequently played out in the Collaborative divorce process. As each struggled not only with the obvious losses associated with the coming apart of their intact family but also with the loss of their own emotional homeostasis, they sought to reestablish a sense of well-being through a variety of behaviors—many of which were experienced by the team as confusing, difficult, or overwhelming.

When Isabel's projected need for stability and security could no longer land successfully on Alan (because he was now withdrawn from her, and angry), she needed a "new home" to receive that particular projection. Isabel's attorney, a warm, older man, began to experience Isabel's intense reliance on him as exaggerated and burdensome. At the same time, Alan's loss of Isabel's admiration meant a loss of the stabilizing belief that he was a desirable man rather than a damaged boy. His disequilibrium played out in the Collaborative process as a hypersensitivity to perceived criticism—particularly when he felt it came from a female team member. We will spend more time exploring the ways in which problematic marital dynamics work their way into the Collaborative process (and Collaborative practitioners) in subsequent chapters.

▼▼▼▼▼
A Note on the Word "Metabolize"

We like this word and use it in this book because it captures one of the fundamental tasks that we ask our clients to perform. The verb "metabolize" comes from the world of biology, and refers to a process in which an organism takes in nutrients and transforms them into useful energy. When we invoke the concept, we are referring to the moments in which we ask our clients to take raw experience or information and transform it, through self-reflection, into a higher-order concept that includes insight and perspective. Metabolized ideas move individuals and the process forward because they are carefully conceived and take into account the perspective of an "other."

▼▼▼▼▼
Lock and Key Dynamics

If your client says "My husband gets furious whenever I spend money; he's stingy," you need to reflect on the question "Where does my client fall on the continuum of emotional entitlement and dependency?" If her husband says "She's a spendthrift, earns nothing, and drains me emotionally and financially," you need to ask yourself, "Is he a controlling provider who has a hard time confronting his wife but seethes silently?" In other words: we want you to begin to reflexively wonder how your client's characteristic complaints represent a Key that fits his or her partner's Lock.

Remember: no matter what picture your client paints of his or her spouse, it can only be fully understood when considered in the context of marriage. Relationships are complicated and formed along many lines. Each couple's dynamic contains many Locks and many Keys. Below are a few simplified examples of typical manifestations of Lock and Key dynamics that we often see in our Collaborative work:

- Passive marries Aggressive
- Sexual/Exciting marries Stable/Staid
- Disorganized/Impulsive marries Organized/Compulsive
- Dependent marries Caretaker
- Nurturing/Needy marries Detached/Independent
- Analytic marries Creative
- Spendthrift marries Miser

THE COLLABORATIVE CONTAINER 3

If you have taken even one introductory Collaborative Practice course, you have heard the term "container" many times. This is a reference to the special environment we create in which clients are able to do the hard work we ask of them. The container has many interrelated components, both structural and psychological. By now, you are likely familiar with the essential procedural components of a Collaborative case,[1] and we will discuss the psychological aspects of each component in detail in Chapter 6. But for now we would like you to think about the theoretical basis for the concept of a Collaborative container.

When we think of the word "container" in a colloquial context, we think of a static object holding something physical, tangible, and measurable. In our context, we use the word metaphorically. Our metaphoric container is not static. It is sturdy, but elastic. Because it is well-designed, it can withstand powerful

---

[1] For an excellent summary of the "flow" of a Collaborative case, read Pauline Tesler's *Collaborative Law: Achieving Effective Resolution in Divorce Without Litigation*, 2nd Edition.

attacks, from both within and without. But it is flexible too, capable, when necessary, of expanding, contracting, or changing shape to accommodate those within its boundaries.

In this book, we want to broaden and deepen our understanding of the Collaborative container as being composed of two inter-related parts—the "Macrocontainer" and the "Microcontainer." The Macrocontainer is the traditional Collaborative container that we have all thought and learned about. It is composed of the Collaborative protocols (as well as thoughtful departures from them), the team itself, and the quality of relationships between and among team members. The authors like to think of the Macrocontainer as offering a warm and strong "arms around" experience. If we think of the healthy mother and baby relationship that we described in Chapter 1, the Macrocontainer would be like the safe environment offered by the father or partner (as well as by extended family and friends) that freed up the mother and supported her in offering the baby her entire empathic attention. The Microcontainer, on the other hand, is analogous to the mother–baby relationship itself. In that relationship, the mother is entirely focused on taking in, tolerating, and helping her baby to make sense of his or her experience. In Collaborative Practice, the Microcontainer is most obviously represented by the emotional support offered to a client by a member of his or her professional team. But there are equally important Microcontainers throughout the team. Think of the times you have leaned on a Collaborative team member for support in managing your anger with a difficult client. It is these relationships and their special qualities (we'll get to those) that make it possible for us and our clients to tolerate the powerful affects that are stirred up during the course of our work.

The Macrocontainer and the Microcontainer are equally important. Without a well-functioning Macrocontainer, the Micro-container could not exist. Just as a mother cannot parent well without a well-functioning emotional and physical support system, you cannot be fully focused on your client or colleague in the ways you need to be without the support of the Collaborative structure and a well-functioning team. Together these two levels of containment, the Macro and the Micro, provide a safe psychological space in which we and our clients can manage the challenges we face.

THE COLLABORATIVE CONTAINER

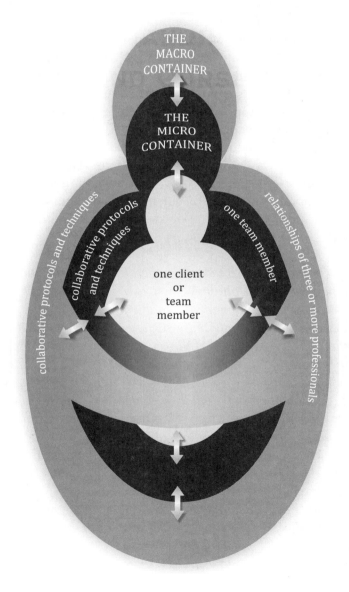

THE
MACRO
CONTAINER

THE
MICRO
CONTAINER

collaborative protocols and techniques

collaborative protocols
and techniques

one client
or
team
member

one team member

relationships of three or more professionals

 arrows indicate emotional interaction

The Macro- and Microcontainers are actually simplified models. In practice they are interrelated and interdependent. For example, departures from standard protocol (changes in the Macrocontainer) must be processed in the relationship between the client and his or her Collaborative professional (the Microcontainer). Similarly, difficulties in, say, the relationship between a client and his attorney (the Microcontainer) must be worked through by the whole team (the Macrocontainer). Also, the distinction between the container and the contained is often blurred, since the relationship between the two contains elements of mutuality. For example, while it is your job (within the Microcontainer) to understand and be supportive of your client, you also learn from and are transformed by him or her.

So why do these distinctions matter at all? What are their practical applications? We think the concepts of Macro- and Microcontainers are useful because they offer a theoretical framework for thinking about the needs of our individual clients, larger process issues, and the interaction of the two. Consider the following example:

Anthony and Theresa, recently separated, hired a Collaborative team composed of two attorneys and two coaches. At the time of their separation, Anthony had six months of sobriety under his belt. He felt betrayed that his wife had asked for the divorce "just as [he] was getting his life together." Theresa said that while Anthony had always been angry, emotionally abusive, and financially controlling, his behavior actually became worse after he stopped drinking. Lately, she said, Anthony had been wildly disorganized, unable to manage caring for their young son (so that she never got a break), unable to tolerate normal amounts of discord, and "constantly on her case" for minor infractions. The final straw came when, during an afternoon outing with their son, Anthony called the child a "little bastard" when the child refused to put on his coat.

Both clients came willingly into the Collaborative process. While they were highly anxious about the outcome of their financial settlement (Anthony had significant family money, Theresa had no assets of her own), they expressed a shared desire to work things out in the best way for their child. In early meetings the coaches and attorneys helped the clients to work out an interim access schedule and short-term answers to the couple's cash-flow concerns.

It soon became clear, however, that Anthony would have tremendous difficulty working within the Collaborative framework. No amount of supportive work on the part of his attorney and coach could help him calm down and wait for the appropriate time in the process to address division of assets. Anthony was chronically late for pickups and drop-offs of his son (often as late as two hours). He was late, too, to Collaborative meetings, with the result that little work could get done. He verbally attacked the team, accusing them of being inefficient. He barraged his wife with harassing e-mails and provoked arguments in front of their child. When the team helped the clients to put protocols in place to limit the amount of face-to-face contact between the two, Anthony broke the protocols.

Anthony's coach and attorney worked hard to contain him. They empathized with his frustrations at not seeing his son enough, but after brief moments of calm, he would return to raging against his wife and the team about his wife's "doling out parenting time bit by bit." In meetings, Anthony had difficulty remaining focused; he talked too much; and he sometimes sounded paranoid. When the team suggested the use of a child specialist, Anthony heard this as an accusation that he was an unfit parent.

As the process inched forward, Anthony's haranguing phone calls to his attorney became more frequent. She reported to the team that she was kept on the phone for hours at a time trying to manage Anthony's requests, complaints, and concerns. Feeling pressured and anxious herself, Anthony's attorney began to send e-mails to Theresa's attorney with specific proposals and requests for counterproposals. She went so far as to have Anthony send proposals directly to his wife and solicit responses. The results were disastrous. Theresa's attorney became first frustrated and then enraged, as her client became increasingly panicked by Anthony's threats. The team had several telephone conferences to strategize around managing Anthony, but they quickly devolved into shouting matches between the two attorneys. Attempts by the coaches to interpret team dynamics as a reflection of the clients' difficulties were ineffective.

When it seemed that the case would fall apart, the team convened a meeting. With the coaches' help, Anthony's attorney was able to talk about her own history of alcoholism, and how it was causing her to feel protective of Anthony in a way that made it difficult for her to set limits with him. She was able to see that she was overidentified with him, and thus having trouble acknowledging his significant pathology and the need for a full psychiatric workup (something the coaches had been suggesting all along). Anthony's attorney's willingness to allow herself to be vulnerable in this setting softened Theresa's attorney. She was able to talk about the way in which Anthony's attorney's positional stance triggered old feelings connected to her own relationship with a dominating mother, feelings that caused her to react angrily and insistently. That reaction in turn had caused Anthony's attorney to feel besieged by both Anthony and this colleague, and led to her becoming more rigid in her advocacy for Anthony's demands.

Once the attorneys were able to gain some emotional perspective on their own reactions to the clients and to one another, they were able to "reset" and regain their Collaborative composure. This freed the team to empathize with and support Anthony's attorney, who had been feeling alone, overwhelmed, and under siege. The team then redefined Anthony's behavior as a shared problem, and moved from a reactive, divisive mode to one in which they could strategize in a coordinated way about how best to help the couple. Anthony's lawyer was relieved of the feeling that she had to respond to Anthony's demands as if every moment were a crisis, and of the guilt that she could never sate his emotional needs. This gave her the fortitude to set limits on his lengthy calls and e-mails. Anthony responded to his attorney's limit-setting by settling down and displaying an increased capacity to take in the support she offered.

In this example you can see the way in which difficulties in the Microcontainer (a disturbance in Anthony's attorney's capacity to manage her relationship to her client) negatively impacted the Macrocontainer (the team's functioning). When the integrity of the Macrocontainer was reestablished through careful processing of the team relationships and their connections to one client's difficulties, the integrity of the Microcontainer was also reestablished. The case continued to be hard work. But because both containers were strengthened through this metabolizing process, both were able to continue to reinforce and support each other as the process continued to a satisfactory conclusion.

Now that we have defined the Macro- and Microcontainers and explored their interrelatedness and interdependence, let's take a closer look at how we establish each of them. Remember: these are models, and thus not fully descriptive of real-life experience. As you'll learn, components of the Macrocontainer can be found in the Microcontainer and vice versa. Still, we find the distinctions helpful in thinking more deeply about the levels on which we function as Collaborative professionals.

ESTABLISHING THE MACROCONTAINER

1. WORKING WITH TRANSFERENCE AND COUNTERTRANSFERENCE

We debated whether to classify transference and countertransference as aspects of the Macrocontainer or of the Microcontainer. In truth, they are fundamental tenets of Collaborative practice, running through our work on all levels in both helpful and unhelpful ways. We decided to include them here, in the section on the Macrocontainer, precisely because of their primacy. As you read, we ask that you bear in mind that these are in fact universal phenomena, in constant operation on both the Macro and Micro levels of practice.

Transference

Transference is the mental act of treating a new relationship as if it were an old one. It isn't always problematic. When we form relationships, we cope with our natural anxiety by gauging the ways the new person does or doesn't conform to the familiar. Thoughts like, "He's funny, like my brother"

"Transference is the mental act of treating a new relationship as if it were an old one."

or "She isn't Catholic, so she probably won't like me" help us navigate new territory. And transference draws people together; most people choose their spouses based on a familiar resonance.

On the other hand, through transference we can perpetuate old patterns of feeling and behavior that don't serve us well. For example, if you had an uncaring father, you may experience some of your friends that way when they're only guilty of being men you're close to. The problem will be complicated further if you angrily accuse them of not caring about you. They'll withdraw, thereby confirming your fears, and you'll be locked in an unconscious cycle that replicates your early unhappy experiences with your father.

The concept of transference is important in our Collaborative work because it helps us to understand the idiosyncratic ways in which our clients feel and behave. When we wonder things like "Why is my client reacting negatively to me when I'm only trying to help?" or "Why does my client seem hell-bent on rejecting even generous offers from his wife?" it helps to remember that transference is the likely culprit. It takes time to get to know your client well enough to be able to pick out (and even anticipate) his or her particular transferential patterns. But when you are able to see your client's quirky behaviors as reflective of his or her typical modes of relating to the world rather than as personal reactions to you or the process, you can gain an objectivity that will allow you to respond effectively.

> "... when you are able to see your client's quirky behaviors as reflective of his or her typical modes of relating to the world rather than as personal reactions to you or the process, you can gain an objectivity that will allow you to respond effectively."

One point to keep in mind is that transference is an unconscious process. It operates out of our awareness, but it can often be brought into our awareness—and made use of—particularly when someone caring (like a Collaborative team member) points it out. Another point to keep in mind is that transference reactions are intensified in times of stress. In other words, the quirky ways that people normally behave are exaggerated during separation and divorce.

Countertransference

Countertransference is a term that refers to a professional's reactions to his or her client. There are two types of counter-transference: those that the professional brings to the process (and are thus emotionally "owned" by him or her), and those that are induced in the professional by the client.

> "Countertransference is a term that refers to a professional's reactions to his or her client."

Countertransference "Owned" by the Professional

This type of countertransference is simply the transference of the professional to his or her client. Like the clients' transference, it is an unconscious process until such time as self-reflection makes it conscious. Let's look at an example:

Mona was the Collaborative coach for the husband in a case in which there had been marital infidelity by the wife. In team meetings, Mona was strangely partisan. The team experienced her as unnecessarily defensive of her own client's interests. Whenever her client's wife spoke, Mona responded harshly and critically, and her body language communicated a clear dislike.

The rest of the team, who knew Mona well, experienced her behavior as uncharacteristic. The wife's coach, Tony, asked for a meeting with Mona in which he gently called attention to the problem of Mona's apparent dislike of the wife. Through a sensitive discussion, Mona was able to own her feelings about the wife. She was also able to trace her feelings to a long-held resentment of her own father, who had left Mona's mother following an affair—leaving Mona and her siblings abandoned and devastated. Once Mona was able to make this connection, she was able to recognize the ways in which her own early experience, which she had never fully faced and worked through, was contributing to a negative countertransference toward her client's wife.

An important point about this type of countertransference is that even though it can be momentarily problematic, it is inevitable. At some point in a case all of us will find ourselves responding to our clients or other team members in ways that are not explainable by present circumstances alone. We all have vulnerabilities in our characters, buttons that, when pushed, cause us to behave in regressive ways. The important questions are (1) how many of these buttons do we have, and (2) how quickly can we correct our course when they are pushed? Healthy professionals and healthy teams (as in the above example) correct their course quickly and use countertransference mishaps as an opportunity for growth and development. Less healthy professionals and less healthy teams can be derailed by countertransference problems.

Let's look at another example of professional-owned transference. This time the professional was unable to self-correct, even after caucusing with a coach who tried to help him regain his own equilibrium.

Curt, a seasoned attorney, found his client's wife, Becka, annoying and provocative. While Curt recognized that his own client, Alex, had foibles too, he was able to forgive those. Becka's bossy manner, her tendency to express herself in absolutes ("This is separate property. That's just the way it is!"), and her evident disdain for Alex really got under Curt's skin. Throughout the first half of the meeting, Curt made several increasingly sarcastic comments in reaction to Becka. The tension in the room rose as he said things like "Becka, I'm afraid I have to disagree with you." Then quietly, "Not that it matters to you, of course." At one point, he repeated a comment Becka made, and added "Really? You really just said that?" Becka looked at her coach incredulously and both she and her coach simultaneously called for a break.

Becka's coach quickly spoke with Alex's coach out in the hall, and both concurred that Alex's coach—a male coach who knew Curt better than anyone else on the team—would speak with Curt and try to help him take a look at his own reactions and get some perspective. During this conversation Curt agreed he needed to "bite his tongue" but felt misunderstood and chastised. Due to time constraints, and a push by both clients to reach some decisions during this particular meeting, the team did not take a longer break to caucus all together—a step that might have helped.

During the break, Becka's coach and attorney spoke with Becka. Both apologetically noted Curt's sarcastic reactions, and asked Becka how she felt. She felt unsafe, anxious, and angry at Curt. However, she remained focused on her wish to move ahead in the meeting, and noted that there was actually a lot of agreement between her and Alex. She felt good about several of the options on the flip chart.

When the full team reconvened, Becka surprised everyone by saying, "Curt, I'm sorry for being so intense. I actually think Alex and I are making some progress here." Curt replied stiffly, "No need to apologize," sat down, and studied his file notes.

After the meeting, which ended with several agreements between the clients, Becka told her coach she was stunned that Curt had not apologized to her. "I thought for sure he'd feel bad about his snarky comments and see that I really wanted to compromise with Alex—but I guess he never did."

The inevitability of professional-owned countertransference is a good argument for each of us doing the hard work of getting to know ourselves well. Good psychotherapists know they must undergo significant psychotherapy themselves before they can be effective clinicians. The authors of this book would go so far as to suggest that personal psychotherapy should be placed alongside a basic Collaborative training as a prerequisite for practice.

▼

"The inevitability of professional-owned countertransference is a good argument for each of us doing the hard work of getting to know ourselves well."

Countertransference Induced by the Client

Client-induced countertransferences are all the feelings we have about our clients that are not idiosyncratic to us but stem from characteristics of the clients themselves. For example, clients who are always in crisis, barrage you with telephone calls, and seem unsatisfied even when they get their way are likely to induce in you feelings of anger and frustration. What's interesting, though, is that even if the client is viewed by the entire team as entitled and difficult, the intensity of each team member's reaction will vary. Some team members might find the client's behavior mildly annoying, while others might find it enraging. What accounts for the difference?

One factor influencing the intensity of a client-induced countertransference is proximity. In other words, if you are the client's attorney (on the front lines, receiving the harassing e-mails), you may struggle more than a team member who is only hearing about the behavior through you or experiencing it in a buffered setting (e.g., a team meeting). A more interesting factor relates to our own normal, healthy personalities and value sets. Some of us would have difficulty maintaining empathy for a client as needy as the one described above, but would have less difficulty maintaining empathy for an overtly hostile client. Some of us would feel protective of a needy client, but frightened of a hostile client. Obviously, our comfort or discomfort with particular difficult character traits in our clients stems from our own early experience in relationships.

When it comes to client-induced countertransferences there are some important ideas to keep in mind:

1. It is normal and expectable that our feelings (countertransferences) about our clients will not remain static or stable—they will shift around. The same client toward whom we feel protective on Tuesday may be the very client we want to fire on Wednesday.

2. Team members may have very differing countertransferences to clients (based on the team members' own personalities and values); all will be useful and valid, because . . .

3. Client-induced countertransference is not to be avoided. In fact, it is our most useful Collaborative tool. It is only by getting pulled into strong feelings about our clients and thinking our way out of those feelings toward a calm neutrality that we can be helpful to them. The metabolizing process of using our own introspective capacity and that of our team to transform feelings *about* our clients into understanding *of* our clients is the very process that informs our ongoing work. We will talk more about that in the next chapter.

> "It is only by getting pulled into strong feelings about our clients and thinking our way out of those feelings toward a calm neutrality that we can be helpful."

Transference

- One individual's patterns of emotional reactions and typical ways of relating that are born of that person's own history of interpersonal experiences
- Includes unconscious presumptions about people and relationships that can distort current experience
- An unconscious process

Common Transferences in the Collaborative Process

- Trust
- Mistrust/Paranoia
- Antagonism
- Dependency
- Entitlement
- Indifference
- Disdain
- Idealization

Countertransference

- A helping professional's set of emotional responses to a client/couple/colleague
- Comprised of both reactions that come out of the professional's personal history (professional-owned) and of responses to the client's own idiosyncratic behaviors (client-induced)

Common Countertransferences in Collaborative Process

- Over-identification with one client or team member
- Vilification of one or both clients or one or more team member
- Rescue fantasies (over-functioning)
- Exaggerated sense of urgency
- Hopelessness
- Regression to an adversarial stance

2. USING THE COLLABORATIVE PROTOCOLS

If you are a parent, you know that children thrive on routine. When their lives follow certain organized principles, they feel safe and secure. This is true on both the concrete and emotional levels. Kids do best when their eating and sleep cycles are fairly regular and when the important people in their lives behave in fairly consistent and predictable ways. When they can trust that the adults in their lives will be there when they are needed, children can tolerate normal amounts of chaos and disappointment. But when their lives are unpredictable and the adults in their lives are unreliable, children become anxious and disorganized. Structure, when it's thoughtfully imposed, provides clear boundaries in which children can be freed up to do the playful work of childhood. In other words, it allows them to be themselves.

The structure of the Collaborative process works very much like good parenting. In order to be effective, this structure must be thoughtful and consistent, but not punitively inflexible. As professionals, we are familiar with the landmarks of a Collaborative case (the first team meeting, the development of the Mission Statement, later team meetings, four-ways, debriefing phone calls, etc.) and the dance we do as a particular case unfolds organically. However, until you have lived a Collaborative case, your knowledge of the process is abstract, not experiential. In fact, as some of our newer colleagues have pointed out, until you have completed several Collaborative cases, you "really don't get it." What this means is that our clients, even those who have researched Collaborative practice before they come to a first meeting with us, need to be educated. They need for us to explain, very early on and more than once, the theory and practice of Collaborative work. They need us to help them to anticipate some of the feelings they may have as we go along. And they need us to follow the process as we have described it, departing from it only after thoughtful consideration and in a way we can explain to them. While Collaborative practice is both an art and a science, we don't make it up as we go along and it is not voodoo. Our clients need to feel safe in that knowledge.

3. CONSIDERING YOUR PROFESSIONAL SETTING

The Collaborative literature already offers some great descriptions of the optimal qualities of the Collaborative physical space; we will briefly review them here:

1. A clean, uncluttered, comfortable, and inviting office, relatively free of evidence of work in other cases (especially those related to litigation);
2. For individual meetings, comfortable chairs in which you can sit facing your client (as opposed to speaking to them from across the expanse of a desk);
3. For team meetings, a large (optimally round) table and private spaces for caucusing;
4. Freedom from intrusion (e.g., telephone calls, colleagues entering the space uninvited); and
5. Good two-way soundproofing.

While we certainly agree that the above aspects of the setting are important, we want to encourage Collaborative practitioners to give thoughtful consideration to some more subtle aspects of their professional setting. Remember, your clients will register everything about you and your office space, and you have no way of knowing in advance which aspects of their experience will have positive or negative meaning to them. That lovely moss-colored velvet couch you recently purchased may connote comfort and safety to one client, while for another it might provoke a worry that you are spending too much money on new furniture and thus overcharging them. A client's quirky characteristic response is an important source of data about his or her psychological dynamics. The client who reacts negatively (and personally) to your new couch is likely displaying an aspect of her character that moves quickly to feeling taken advantage of or given short shrift. If you register her response early, you already have a jump on a beginning hypothesis about how she may feel and behave as your work unfolds.

Obviously you can't control every client's response, nor should you try. You are entitled to a certain amount of self-expression in your workplace; after all, you need to feel good working there.

But what you can and should do is present a restrained, professional view of yourself and your personality. Remember, you are inevitably going to draw transferential responses from your client (as in the couch example above). And, as we've described, these responses (as well as your countertransference reactions) are not only inevitable, but crucial to our understanding of our clients. That is the first reason that we encourage you to avoid placing objects in your office that offer too much personal information about you. The most obvious examples are family photographs. That smiling picture of you and your family on a beach vacation may give you pleasure, but it is also a hook for clients to latch on to as they form opinions about you. "So what?" you may ask, "I'm not doing therapy; I don't need to be a blank screen." True, you don't. And, over time, you and your client will learn more about each other. But if, in their early contacts with you, your client is faced with material in your office that puts you in a position of having to answer specific personal questions, you may have muddied the waters between the two of you in such a way that it is more difficult to get a clean snapshot of your client's particular ways of entering into a relationship with you—and that snapshot is important as you begin to assess your client.

The second reason that we counsel colleagues to avoid putting too many photographs and other personally specific items in their offices is that to do so can be experienced by our clients as insensitive. Remember, they are coming to you at a moment in which their worlds have been turned upside down and their families rent asunder; they may feel angry, grieving, lost, lonely, and alienated. This is probably not a time when they are interested in seeing photographs of happy, intact families, nor your daughter's recently won diving trophy—evidence of what they will likely imagine to be your enviably satisfying and stable life.

The third reason that we want you to consider avoiding putting explicitly or pro-

> ▼
>
> "This is not a time when [your clients] are interested in seeing photographs of happy, intact families, nor your daughter's recently won diving trophy. . . They need to know that the time they spend with you is for them and about them— that you are intensely focused on their needs and concerns."

vocatively personal objects in your office is that to do so may, in your clients' minds, move the focus off of them and onto you. Even though an individual client knows that you have other clients and a personal life, they need to feel that while they are with you they are your sole concern. They need to know that the time they spend with you is *for them* and *about them*—that you are intensely focused on their needs and concerns.

This way of thinking about professional neutrality mirrored in our work space will feel more familiar to psychotherapists than to lawyers, financial professionals, and others who work in the field of Collaborative practice. We recognize that some of you may not want to relinquish the personal touches that make an office feel like home. We simply want to encourage the same thoughtfulness in constructing your office setting that you employ in other parts of your work. We don't want to be doctrinaire, but let's face it: one or two photos of your grandkids on your desk placed to face away from your clients may not give you the same pleasure as a wall of family portraits, but it won't disrupt your ability to assess your clients, and it won't upset them, either.

4. HOLDING REGULAR MEETINGS

Because Collaborative meetings are notoriously difficult to schedule (involving many people with busy professional and personal lives trying to carve out time for two-hour meeting plus travel!), we have learned that it is best to schedule several meetings at a time. We know to stress with our clients the importance of regular attendance (meetings are difficult and expensive to reschedule, canceling interferes with the momentum of the case, etc.), doing their homework, and showing up on time. But it's helpful to remind ourselves that, as professionals whose responsibility it is to hold the frame, we need to meet those standards and then some.

It is incumbent on us to arrive at meetings *on time and ready to work*. This means that when the clients arrive you will have readied the meeting space, made copies of any needed documents, and, most importantly, done any preparatory work among and between team members. If you want to chat with colleagues who are also friends, or if you need to do some pre-meeting discussing of the case—schedule it in. Do not keep clients waiting; they are already anxious and may feel awkward sitting alone together in the waiting room. One possible exception might be if a crisis or new critical information about the case surfaces so close to the meeting itself that the team does not have time to process it (either in person or by phone) prior to the meeting. In that case, the team might want to plan to spend, say, a half hour of the meeting time to discuss the issue before bringing the clients into the room. Before spending that half hour, however, team members would need to take a moment to explain the plan to their clients. If the clients felt uncomfortable waiting together, the team might consider asking one of them if they would prefer to wait in an empty office. Thus, your restructuring of the meeting would represent a considered departure from, rather than a break in, the frame.

5.   PAYING ATTENTION TO FEES AND FEE POLICIES

Most people—professionals and clients alike—find it easier to talk about sex than to talk about money. In fact, even though finances are central to our clients' lives, most of our therapist colleagues don't know how much their clients actually earn. So it is not surprising that many of us have trouble being clear, up front, about our fees and our fee policies, collecting fees in a timely way, and knowing what to do if a client gets behind in his or her payments.

It is our experience that of all the professionals on a Collaborative team, mental health professionals often have the most difficulty managing financial issues. Lawyers are often backed up by firms that set fees and fee policies and generate invoices. Even if a lawyer is a solo practitioner, he or she has probably worked in a firm at some point and internalized something of the financial culture. And financial professionals—well, they are more comfortable with the topic than most of the rest of us.

Still, any of us is vulnerable to having complicated or conflictual feelings related to fees, and these feelings are rooted in our own experiences with money. For example, if you grew up in a family in which money was substituted for love, you might struggle with some feelings of guilt when it comes to charging your client for a team phone call. You might tell yourself, "I am supposed to be helping them, this process is really expensive, and they don't have a lot of money." Or, if you grew up angry that you were overbur-

dened with financial responsibility too early, you might find yourself getting angry at a client who is late paying his bill. In the same
way that we must come to this work having spent a good deal of
time exploring the dynamics of our relationships, we must come
having explored our own experience of and feelings about money
and the earning of it.

Above we discussed the importance of being explicit with our
clients about the structure and flow of the Collaborative process.
The same is true of the fees and fee policies of the various members of the team. We believe that team members, as well as clients,
should know the varying fee policies of all the professionals on the
team from the beginning. For example, some professionals charge
for travel to meetings, others do not. When you consider differences in policies and differences in fees (both within and across
disciplines on the team), you can see that *where* a meeting is held
can have significant implications for how much each member of a
couple is charged. The fact that the most expensive member of the
team charges for travel may not necessarily mean that a couple
decides to hold the bulk of their meetings at that professional's
office; perhaps other factors, such as geographical convenience,
are more important. But if these issues are not spelled out early so
that all factors can be kept in mind when meetings are scheduled,
clients may become resentful.

While we can't tell our clients in advance how much their
divorce is going to cost, we can and should tell them what services
they will be charged for. If we are going to charge for weekly team
calls and professional-only meetings, for telephone contact with
our clients, or to read e-mails, we need to tell them at the beginning of our work with them. Mental health professionals making
the switch from psychotherapy to Collaborative Practice may not
be accustomed to charging prorated fees for non-face-to-face services. If you fall in that category, speak to some of your Collaborative colleagues to gather ideas as you set your own policies.

Early in our Collaborative work the authors noticed that the
issue of payment for missed or cancelled meetings was rarely, if
ever, discussed among team members or with clients. When we
explored the issue a bit, we learned that attorneys do not charge
for appointments cancelled by clients. When we asked our legal

colleagues about this, they explained that if a client cancels, they are able to fill the time with work for other clients. As mental health professionals, however, the authors do need a cancellation policy—both of us charge our clients the full fee for a session that they cancel less than 48 hours in advance. We need this policy, because if our client cancels we cannot fill that time with other billable work. We have discussed this issue with colleagues in other disciplines. Now our legal and financial teammates are comfortable with our policy of charging for late-cancelled meetings, even if they do not charge themselves. Of course, we do not charge if *the professionals* decide to cancel a scheduled meeting. The important point is not that we all charge the same fee or have the same policies; it is that these issues are talked about and made explicit up front.

Other important money-related topics that inevitably come up in Collaborative cases are the questions of retainers and collection of fees. Attorneys (and some financial neutrals) come to this work already comfortable with the idea of charging retainers. For us "mentals," this is usually a new concept. Each team member needs to be clear about his or her own expectations. How much is your original retainer? At what point do you expect it to be replenished? The team may make a considered decision to break from policy. For example, in practice we find that the replenishment of a retainer becomes an issue for ongoing team discussion, since it may be interwoven with other financial issues that the couple is grappling with. Where is the money to pay for the process coming from—cash? a loan against a retirement account? It may take time to free up those assets, and the team may decide to "float" the couple while arrangements are made.

Still, no professional on the team should feel pressured to lower his or her fee to accommodate a struggling couple or to delay being paid to accommodate the process. While we are in a helping profession, it is still a job. We deserve and need to get paid in a way that is comfortable for us. If we undercharge or carry our clients' debt, we are in essence subsidizing their process. We are likely to feel exploited, and will not be emotionally free to offer our clients the best service possible. Also, allowing our clients to get in hock to us does them a disservice by either (1) enabling a pattern of exploitation of others or (2) putting them in a position where they may feel guilty or anxious, and thus unable to fully participate in the Collaborative process.

ESTABLISHING THE MICROCONTAINER

As we've explained, the Microcontainer is dyadic; it is composed of two people. As with any intimate relationship, it contains aspects of mutuality. But the client/professional relationship in Collaborative Practice has special characteristics. Let's take a look at them.

1. STAYING IN ROLE

Mental health professionals, regardless of whether they are engaged in psychotherapy or Collaborative practice, are bound by an ethical code that does not allow them to have an outside relationship of any kind with their client, even if the "work" with their client is completed. There are good reasons for this injunction, and we believe it should apply to all professionals engaged in Collaborative Practice. First, even though the Collaborative practitioner is hired by the client, there is a perceived power imbalance. Clients are dependant on us, so they need to be able to see us as powerful—knowledgeable, strong, and capable of helping. Because of this, clients often idealize their Collaborative professionals a bit, and are therefore vulnerable to being exploited, hurt, or seduced into interactions they might not otherwise seek out. At the same time, this idealization may cause clients to push at the boundaries of the professional/client relationship, in an attempt to get more *of* and *from* us. It then becomes increasingly incumbent on us to maintain the boundaries of our role. If we get pulled into another type of relationship with our client, we lose the intellectual neutrality we need if we are to be helpful to them.

And that brings us to the second reason that it is crucial that we stay in our role, even after a case is completed. We have heard of cases in which Collaborative professionals have become good friends with or even hired their former clients as employees. When we sign a Collaborative Participation Agreement, we are saying

▼

"When we sign a Collaborative Participation Agreement we are saying 'I am your Collaborative professional in perpetuity—I am here for you for as long and whenever you need me.'"

"I am your Collaborative professional in *perpetuity*—I am here for you for as long as and whenever you need me." And it's true; the divorce doesn't end at the signing of an Agreement. Rather, that's when it begins. Clients may come back to us at various intervals for many years, perhaps to revisit or talk through some aspect of their Agreement or to discuss a new issue in their co-parenting relationship. We know that non–mental health professionals are not bound by the same ethical injunctions that bind mental health professionals. Still, the authors don't think it's going too far to say that to step out of role with your Collaborative client is unethical, since it hinders your ability to be helpful to them going forward.

2. MAINTAINING A CLIENT-CENTERED APPROACH

This point is closely related to the one above. Remember: The Collaborative professional-to-client relationship is often intense and mutually affecting, but it is not an equal one. We all have bad days, but our clients don't need to know it. Keep your clients' goals front and center.

3. KEEPING SMALL TALK TO A MINIMUM

Our clients are usually anxious going into Collaborative meetings, especially in the beginning. It is tempting to want to banter about seemingly neutral topics in an attempt to put them at ease. Also, it's hard not to chat with our colleagues—we often are genuinely pleased to see each other, and the pull is strong to ask whether a team member enjoyed his recent birthday party, or to report how our 11th grader is doing with his college essays. We even attended a meeting where one professional announced that it was her 25th wedding anniversary—yikes! Remember: For most clients, these meetings are somber affairs. Our "small talk" can easily translate as insensitivity or worse.

We certainly realize that as the Collaborative process moves along you will get to know your clients better and develop an easier and more comfortable rapport with them. You'll learn which clients are actively angry or grieving and need you to stay completely focused on them and the task at hand, and which are actually made more comfortable by peripheral chat. We are definitely not suggesting that you abandon your sense of humor or your playfulness. Those qualities are often critical in our work. We are simply suggesting that, at least at first, less is more. Hold back until you know your clients well enough to "read" them, then you'll be able to match your demeanor to their needs.

4. BEING ENTHUSIASTIC ABOUT THE COLLABORATIVE PROCESS, BUT NOT CELEBRATORY

In first team meetings, it is common for the professionals to introduce themselves and to say a bit about what drew them to Collaborative Practice and how they hope to be helpful to the couple. Watch your language here. Avoid such phrases as "I'm so excited you've chosen this process," "I'm really looking forward to working with you," or "The beauty of Collaborative is . . ." We know you mean well, but even though our clients may have mature goals for the process, to them (at least early on) there is nothing exciting, fun, or beautiful about it. As one client darkly put it to an inappropriately cheery team, "I'm glad you are all so hopped up about the dismantling of my life."

5. LISTENING NONJUDGMENTALLY

In working with divorcing clients we hear a lot of stories, and some of them are not pretty. Regardless of your own feelings about, say, people who cheat or move out without telling their children in advance, there is no place in Collaborative Practice for judgment or proselytizing. If you feel shocked or dismayed by what your client tells you about how his or her spouse has behaved, remember: there are two sides to every story. You won't know the nuances for some time. Be supportive, but not quick to jump on the bashing bandwagon. And if you feel shocked or dismayed by something your own client has done, try to hold on to the idea that the behavior occurred in the context of a bad marriage. The two were very likely in it together. If you can't do that, practice your poker face.

6. CONVEYING EMPATHY (VERSUS SYMPATHY)

It's counterintuitive, but sometimes our attempts to be supportive of our clients can actually make them feel worse. For example, if a client tells us that he has discovered evidence of an online affair on his wife's computer and you gasp and say, "Oh gosh, what a nightmare! I feel so bad for you!" you may unintentionally intensify the painful feelings your client is already experiencing by magnifying the horror of the incident. You also may accidentally add to his shame or unintentionally convey that this situation is overwhelming to you. As another example, imagine a client who begins to weep as she discloses that her husband is dating a much younger woman. Say you respond, "I know just how you feel! That just happened to my neighbor!" The difficulty with this response, as with the previous example, is that it relates to *your* experiences and shifts the focus of the discourse away from the client and onto you. These are sympathetic responses, and might convey that you feel sorry for your client. But your clients can get sympathy from their friends; they need something more from you. They need empathy.

▼

"Empathy is critical, because what comforts anyone most is the experience of feeling profoundly understood."

Empathy is the capacity to really know what it means to walk in your client's shoes, to *get* your client on a gut level. Empathy is critical, because what comforts anyone most is the experience of feeling profoundly understood. The expression of empathy takes many forms. Sometimes empathy comes in the form of a heartfelt (but measured) expression of concern, such as "That must be very painful for you." Sometimes it comes in the form of a nonverbal communication of focused interest, such as maintaining eye contact, or leaning in toward your client. How do we develop empathy with a particular client? By talking less and listening more. Regardless of your discipline, the first thing you must do with every client is to listen to his or her story and really *take it in*.

7. SETTING LIMITS

Sometimes our clients either do not have or have temporarily lost the ability to regulate their own behavior. Clients who persist in denigrating their spouses, sticking to "positions" rather than being willing to consider options, or acting out in various other ways (not doing their homework, canceling meetings, e-mailing their spouse's attorney without including the rest of the team, etc.) need us to rein them in. You'll couch your language in a way that fits your understanding of your client's personality and needs—perhaps you'll use a gentle verbal "nudge" or a humorous chiding. Regardless, the message is the same: "This isn't helpful; cut it out."

8. RESPECTING SILENCE

One of the hardest things to do is to say nothing when someone is suffering. Still, restraint is often the most powerfully helpful stance you can adopt. If your client is weeping as she speaks about her feelings of loneliness and devastation and you are able to sit quietly, *take in*, and *tolerate* her powerful affects without moving in too quickly

> "Sitting in silence with someone who is expressing powerfully painful affect while remaining acutely *tuned in* . . . is a powerfully therapeutic act."

to help, you are not doing nothing. Sitting in silence with someone who is expressing powerfully painful affect while remaining acutely *tuned in* can feel almost athletically difficult. But being able to be with a client in her pain without resorting to "there-there's" is a powerfully therapeutic act.

We have all been in meetings where it occurs to us that the professionals are doing most of the talking, generating all of the options, or crowding the clients out in a variety of other ways. When that happens, it can be extremely useful to simply point out the phenomenon to the team and wonder aloud as to the reason. When a team (or one member of the team) is overfunctioning in that way, it is usually because someone or everyone in the room is protecting the clients from doing their own work—which may include struggling with painful feelings or difficult impasses.

▼

"If we don't allow a silence to develop, we will lose a potentially important opportunity for deeper understanding, and may rob our clients of the opportunity to do their own work."

Another reason we should practice being quiet is that not all silences are alike. If we rush in to fill what we perceive as a void, we lose the opportunity to understand what is contained in any particular silence. Is the room quiet because both clients are working through grief? Is one or both of them worried about saying something that will provoke the other? Is one of them feeling so angry that she is afraid that if she speaks at all she will launch into a diatribe? Are both clients actually actively considering options in their heads? There are as many meanings for silence as there are silences themselves. The point is, if we don't allow a silence to develop we will lose a potentially important opportunity for deeper understanding, and may rob our clients of the opportunity to do their own work.

9.   USING REALITY TESTING

There will be times during the course of your work with a client when you will feel that he has lost perspective. Perhaps you see him projecting an aspect of himself into a team member so that he sees that team member as persecuting him when the reality doesn't bear that out. Perhaps your client is clinging to the hope that she can keep the family home when there is no viable option for that. Perhaps your client, in a moment of anger, has temporarily lost sight of the fact that his soon-to-be-ex is actually a good mother. It is your job to then gently redirect your clients, to point out that while you can empathize with how they might be feeling under these conditions of stress, you do not see things the way they do. If your client is relatively healthy and has developed trust in you, he or she will be able to regain a more reality-based point of view.

10.   USING PARAPHRASING AND REFRAMING

Paraphrasing is one of the most basic building blocks of an empathic response. When we mirror our clients' words, closely following their language and thought content, we are explicitly illustrating our interest in and our determination to accurately hear and integrate their experience and perspective. Paraphrasing is a way to say to our client "I am here, I am listening, and I get it."

While paraphrasing is a building block for the creation of empathy, reframing is a building block for reality testing. At first blush reframing may look much like paraphrasing, but it is significantly different. Reframing is the verbal act of restating something our client has said with a slight shift toward a more rational, reasonable, or balanced point of view. When we offer a reframe, our message is "I am here. I am listening, and let me offer a slightly different perspective that might move you forward a step or two." Here's an example. Let's say your client asserts "My husband is such a slob, I just know my kids will develop terrible habits from spending time at his house." A paraphrase might be: "You sound really worried that your children may turn into slobs like your husband." A reframe might be: "You and your husband are different in some ways; it sounds hard to trust that he will work as hard as you will to instill good habits in your children." Do you hear the difference? While the first example might be best when you feel it essential to let your client know you are right there with her, the second would be more effective if you were working delicately to help your client give her husband the benefit of the doubt. Reframing is like reaching out a hand to gently pull your client in a new, healthier direction.

11. MAKING LINKS

When we talk about the transformative potential of a Collaborative divorce, we are referring to the ways our clients use the process to gain a deeper understanding of themselves and their old patterns of relating so that they will be free to make new and better choices in the future. Along the way, they will have necessarily gained an appreciation of their own contribution to their marital difficulties, and an enhanced capacity to see their spouse (and hence, all others) in three dimensions.

One of the tools that we have to help our clients to not only *survive* but actually *grow* as they move through the Collaborative process is helping them to make links, or mental connections, between old experience and current behavior or ways of feeling.

For example, we might point out to a client that his fear of being left destitute by his divorce is really a reflection of having been raised by parents who survived the Great Depression. We might help a mother to recognize that her anxiety at sharing custody with her children's father is more closely related to her own experience of having had an overwhelmed Dad than to her husband's parenting capacities.

The idea of making links for clients may seem difficult, complicated, or daunting. In reality, we all do it for our clients every day. Telling a client "Okay, so once again you're thinking your husband wants to leave you homeless. We've talked about how he's actually more anxious than vindictive" is not a particularly deep intervention, but it's a great example of making links by pointing out patterns within the process. As a deeper example, consider the following vignette:

Amy, already well into the Collaborative process, was planning to move out of the marital home into a new, smaller one. After spending Friday touring houses with a realtor, Amy called her coach on a Monday morning. She described having spent the weekend in what she described as a "terrifying, dark place." She was baffled by how depressed she felt after seeing potential new homes, and by the repetitive intrusive thoughts she had been having of terrible things happening to her young children.

The coach, already familiar with her client's history, knew that Amy had been raised by her mother, who had died the year Amy graduated from college. Alone in the world, Amy had fought off feelings of devastation and panic by moving into action. She quickly sold her childhood home and bought a smaller one that she could manage. She married her husband soon after, hoping to regain a sense of safety.

With some help from her coach, Amy was able to see the way in which she had been warding off the grief associated with her impending divorce in the same way she had fled from the overwhelming grief associated with the earlier loss of her mother. The practical act of looking at houses in which she would live alone not only brought the reality of her current situation alive, but also triggered the feelings that Amy had felt in association with the loss of her childhood home—feelings that, at the time, had been too overwhelming to face and work through. Amy also could be brought to see that her unrealistic yet powerfully torturous recurrent bouts of panic about losing her children were connected to the early loss of her mother.

Once Amy was able to make a link between her current depression and anxiety and her earlier overwhelming losses, she felt much better. She came to her next Collaborative meeting better able to face her grief about the divorce and, hence, better able to work. She had also been given fodder for her individual therapy.

▼▼▼▼▼

A Word on the Macrocontainer, the Microcontainer, and the Team Model

The concepts of the Microcontainer and the Macrocontainer help us to understand the power and importance of a team model of practice. Think about it: in a team comprised of only two attorneys and two clients, you do have Microcontainers for each of the clients (their attorneys). Assuming that the two attorneys trust each other enough for open communication and are well–trained, you also have a small Macrocontainer for difficulty in either of the client-to-professional relationships (each professional can support the other). That Macrocontainer

▼

"The [purpose of] the Macrocontainer is to use the intellectual, supportive, and metabolizing function of several professionals in supporting the intense work that is happening between a professional and his or her client."

is a bit flimsy, however. If there is a difficult dynamic in one of the client-to-professional relationships, that dynamic will very likely rear its head in the professional-to-professional-relationship. Then what? It takes very skilled, very self-aware professionals to be able to sort out powerful and complex projections, transferences, and countertransferences in their relationship to each other in such a way that they can make use of their new understanding to move the case forward. That's what the Macrocontainer is for—to use the intellectual, supportive, and metabolizing functions of several professionals in supporting the intense work that is happening between a professional and his or her client.

ASSESSMENT AND INTERVENTION: THE RIGIDITY/FLEXIBILITY CONTINUUM

4

A CONTINUUM MODEL OF TRANSFORMATIVE CAPACITY

Those of us who have done at least a few Collaborative cases know that not all are equally satisfying. At one end of the spectrum are the cases that we have come to call "transformative," where each member of the couple emerges from the process like a butterfly from a chrysalis—with an enhanced self-awareness and capacity for empathy, ready to make new and different life decisions, and poised to take advantage of the unanticipated opportunities that this life transition affords. However difficult their process may have felt at times, these clients have been able, through the healthy flexibility of their characters, to recover from the dark moments. At the other end of the spectrum are what the authors have darkly come to refer to as the "get 'er dones." These are the "non-transformative" cases, the ones in which both parties never move on from their original stances. Try as we may, even the most experienced among us are unable to help these clients to budge from their polarized positions. Rageful, grieving, angry, seeking retribution, indifferent—whatever difficult emotional stance they had when they came into the process they carry throughout and are unable to relinquish. Sometimes these cases terminate prematurely; one client simply stomps off in a huff. But if we can hold them in the process to the end, if we can keep them out of the potential bloodbath of litigation long enough to reach agreement, we have done our jobs successfully.

Most of our cases fall somewhere between the two poles of the spectrum between "transformative" and "non-transformative." Sometimes one member of the couple grows psychologically through the process while the other remains stuck. Sometimes both members of the couple are able to grow in certain areas but remain stuck in others. Usually, even when both members of the couple are generally pleased with the final product, they feel battered and bruised by certain aspects of the experience and resentful about some of the compromises they have made (albeit willingly). Also, since recovery from the divorce process often takes many years, feelings about the Collaborative process itself and the capacity to learn from it do not freeze at the moment the clients sign their Agreement. A healthier client will make evolving use, over time, of what he or she has internalized during the Collaborative process. What determines where a client, or a couple, falls on this spectrum? We suggest that it is the level of psychological health or ill-health—in other words, flexibility or rigidity—within the characters of each.

In Chapter 1 we discussed the fact that when we experience early trauma we must employ defenses (such as denial, repression, or minimization) to keep the feelings about those experiences at bay. We made the point that the more psychic energy we must expend in employing these defenses, the less energy is left over for other uses. Finally, we explained that an individual who must make heavy use of defenses has a more limited, caricatured, or rigid way of relating to the world. The latter individuals are the ones we often refer to as "character disordered." They are typically unable to see things from another person's point of view and are resistant to change. They are our most difficult Collaborative clients.

THE RIGIDITY/FLEXIBILITY CONTINUUM: A NEW CONCEPT

As we've discussed, all of us utilize defenses to some degree. The important question is not "Do we ever act in irrationally rigid ways?" Rather, it is "How often?" and "How quickly are we able to recover?" In other words, characterological rigidity and flexibility exist on a continuum; we all move along it. In times of stress (such as early on in a divorce, or at difficult moments along the way) our feelings and behaviors may place us at the rigid end. In better times we may land closer to the

> "The important question is not 'Do we ever act in irrationally rigid ways?' Rather, it is 'How often?' and 'How quickly are we able to recover?' . . . The quicker you can separate your client's more rigid behaviors under stress from where his behaviors generally cluster over time, the quicker you can develop realistic goals for your client in his Collaborative process."

flexible end. It takes time to get to know our clients. Where their behaviors will "cluster" along the continuum is often not apparent at the start of a case. What you'll notice is that the more rigid a client, the more strain will be experienced in both the Macrocontainer and Microcontainer. You'll have to work harder, and fewer techniques will be successful in moving things along. We have learned the hard way that the sooner we can assess our clients (locate their characters along what we call the Rigidity/Flexibility Continuum) the better, because certain techniques, while they might work beautifully with a more flexible client, will have disastrous results with a rigid client.

We've also noticed that early assessment is important to team morale. The quicker you can separate your client's more rigid behaviors *under stress* from where his behaviors *generally cluster* over time, the quicker you can develop realistic goals for your client in his Collaborative process. We are not advocating setting the bar too low, but we are suggesting that setting it too high can set up the professionals for disappointment and frustration and can get in the way of meeting clients *where they really are.*

THE RIGIDITY/FLEXIBILITY CONTINUUM

Rigidity ⟷ Flexibility

Significant Pathology ⟷ Relative Health

Non-Transformative ⟷ Transformative

COMMON MANIFESTATIONS OF THE RIGIDITY/FLEXIBILITY CONTINUUM

Positionality ⟷ Willingness to consider options

Lack of insight ⟷ Self-reflection/Insight

Blame/Projection ⟷ Ownership/Perspective

Anger/Vengefulness ⟷ Forgiveness

Entitlement/Self-absorption ⟷ Generosity

Victimization/Passivity ⟷ Volition/Empowerment

Catastrophizing ⟷ Hope

USING THE CONTINUUM TO ADAPT OUR TECHNIQUES TO INDIVIDUAL CLIENTS

In the last chapter, we discussed some specific techniques that we use with clients. Let's quickly review them here, and think about whether they might be appropriate for use with either rigid or flexible clients. Then we'll look at some illustrative vignettes.

1. STAYING IN ROLE, MINIMIZING SMALL TALK, NOT TREATING THE PROCESS AS CELEBRATORY/ MAINTAINING A CLIENT FOCUS

The more traumatized and fragile a client, the more self-absorbed. Highly rigid clients will be hypersensitive to feeling that you don't take their pain seriously, and exquisitely attuned to moments when they may lose your undivided attention. While they are likely to be the ones who push hardest against your boundaries, they are the ones who need boundaries the most. So while maintaining a professional stance is important for every client, a rigid client is likely to be less forgiving of your lapses than a flexible one.

2.   NONJUDGMENTAL LISTENING

Again, this is important for all clients. But if a rigid client even smells a negative judgment coming off of you, watch out.

3.   EMPATHY

All clients need to feel understood. But flexible clients will be able to bounce back if you fail to empathize with them at an important moment or say something that does not resonate with their experience (in other words, you get it wrong). More rigid clients may react disproportionately—even disastrously—to such inevitable failures on our part. They may feel we've suddenly emotionally abandoned them. They may view our human frailties as evidence of not caring about them or of being incompetent. Also, while all clients require empathy from us (and will require more of it at the beginning and during difficult times in the process), the most rigid clients need it *all the time.*

4.   LIMIT SETTING

We've been developing the idea that the more psychologically unhealthy a client is, the more likely he or she is to hold on to the same (often distorted) ideas about his or her spouse over time, and to behave in repeatedly difficult ways over the course of the Collaborative process. It stands to reason, then, that while even our healthy clients will need limits at stressful points in the process, our more rigid clients will need stronger limits more often.

5.   SILENCE

We've talked about the importance of allowing silence in order to give ourselves time to develop understanding and to afford our clients the space to reflect and struggle a bit to do their own work. While even healthy clients may at times push us to fill the void, they can usually appreciate the importance of our not doing so and can come to find our restraint helpful. More rigid clients, however, are likely to find silence intolerable.

6.   REALITY TESTING

Clients who fall closer to the flexible end of our Continuum will be able to make good use of reality testing; they will come to be grateful for it as an important tool for developing insight about themselves. Rigid clients, on the other hand, will reject your differing point of view out of hand, and will see your daring to speak a different truth as a failure of empathy.

7.   PARAPHRASING AND REFRAMING

By now you're seeing the pattern. While healthier clients will be interested in our putting a new spin on their perceptions, very rigid clients will simply want to see their own point of view mirrored, quite literally, back to them. They want to know that you "get it" in the exact way they mean it. Reframing of their ideas will be anathema to them. And even when you paraphrase, you'd better be careful to stick closely to their words. If you get it wrong, they'll notice.

8.   MAKING LINKS

As we discussed in the previous chapter, making links between past and present experience is crucial for clients who are able to make transformative use of the Collaborative experience. On the other hand, rigid clients will experience your attempts to point out the ways that their current feelings or behaviors are informed by, or replicate, their earlier patterns as evidence that you wish to minimize the validity and reality of their current suffering.

TECHNIQUES FOR WORKING WITH CLIENTS ALONG THE CONTINUUM

Rigidity	⟷	**Flexibility**
Significant Pathology	⟷	**Relative Health**
Non-Transformative	⟷	**Transformative**
Staying in role	⟷	Staying in role
Minimizing small talk	⟷	Minimizing small talk
Not acting celebratory	⟷	Not acting celebratory
Nonjudgmental listening	⟷	Nonjudgmental listening

$$\begin{array}{rcl}
\text{Empathy} & \longleftrightarrow & \text{Empathy} \\
\text{Paraphrasing} & \longleftrightarrow & \text{Paraphrasing} \\
\text{Limit setting} & \longleftrightarrow & \text{Limit setting} \\
& & \text{Use of silence} \\
& & \text{Reality testing} \\
& & \text{Reframing} \\
& & \text{Making links}
\end{array}$$

WORKING WITH CLIENTS ALONG THE CONTINUUM: THREE VIGNETTES

Here are some short vignettes describing clients at various points on the Continuum. As you read, you will see that as our clients move further away from a healthy flexibility and closer to an unhealthy rigidity, our repertoire of helpful techniques and the possibility of transformative experience shrink rapidly.

The Flexible Client

Tom and Richard, the parents of twin boys, were working on their access plan with their coaches. Tom, who had been the primary breadwinner (and therefore had spent less time with the boys than had Richard), was insistent that the boys spend exactly 50 percent of their time with each parent after the divorce. Richard was supportive of Tom having a full relationship with their children, but both he and the coaches could see that Tom's work schedule would not realistically allow him to care for the children more than three nights per week. With help from the coaches (empathizing with his anxiety while reframing his stated interests, exploring the children's needs in greater depth, helping him take in and acknowledge Richard's assurance that he supported the children's attachment to him), Tom was able to see that his insistence on an equal weekly timeshare reflected a worry that he was not as important to his children as was Richard. When his coach made the link between Tom's worry and his childhood experience, Tom was even able to connect this concern to his boyhood relationship with his own father, who had worked long hours and rarely spent time with his son. Once Tom recognized the historical roots of his present-day concern that he would be margin-

alized in the rearing of his boys, he felt reassured. He and Richard were able to work out a weekly schedule in which Tom had the boys for three overnights per week. Richard was happy to facilitate Tom spending extended periods with the boys over school breaks and summer vacation—times Tom could take time off from work. Both clients experienced this discussion as an important moment; Tom gained insight into some of the motivations driving his parenting decisions, Richard felt Tom was able to see him as a supportive co-parent despite the general acrimony between them, and both could see the ways their co-parenting relationship was strengthened by the process.

The Moderately Rigid Client

Andrea and Phillip were in the process of resolving their cash flow concerns. Despite an agreement to avoid discussing the process with Phillip outside of Collaborative meetings, Andrea persisted in sending her husband frequent e-mails containing "proposals" for ways they could resolve their disputes. When the team first addressed this behavior in a meeting, Andrea acknowledged having gone outside the process, but proclaimed: "Look, I know I'm not 'supposed' to do this. But I am an adult, and no one can tell me how and when to talk to my husband." Andrea experienced the team as having "chided" her. She continued to e-mail her husband between meetings, even going so far as to ask him if he thought they could work out the finances more cheaply on their own. After some individual work with him, Phillip's coach encouraged him to express his feelings about Andrea's behavior. At the next team meeting he said, "It makes me really uncomfortable, Andrea, when you try to engage me in substantive financial discussions between team meetings. You know I don't like conflict, and I worry that you are trying to strong-arm me into agreeing to something that isn't in my best interest. I want to keep all our financial discussions within the Collaborative process where they belong." Upon hearing this, Andrea acknowledged Phillip's concern and promised to stop e-mailing him about things related to their divorce. However, immediately following the meeting, Andrea called her attorney to complain that Phillip was being "a baby," and that it was ridiculous that she was being discouraged from speaking to him between meetings. The team set up another phone conversation between Andrea, her coach, and her attorney. The professionals clearly delineated for Andrea which topics were safe for her to e-mail Phillip about and which were not. While they offered Andrea empathy for her frustration, they focused on limit setting. They understood that Andrea was not capable of developing insight into her own behavior, but felt she was motivated to make the process work and could follow clear protocols. After that, while Andrea's behavior wasn't perfect (she still sent the occasional inappropriate e-mail), she pushed at the boundaries of the process much less frequently. Over time, as she developed more trust in her team (and in Phillip), she stopped trying to circumvent the process. She regressed to earlier behaviors only at particularly stressful moments in the process.

The Rigid Client

Brian and Jennifer had been working with their Collaborative team for six months. Brian's early assertions that his wife was abusive and out to "screw" him financially had not been borne out over the course of the work, but Brian held steadfastly to these notions. One day, Brian forwarded an e-mail to his coach that, he insisted, constituted hard evidence that Jennifer intended to bankrupt him. The coach reviewed the e-mail, which, it turned out, was simply a response to Brian's own inquiry as to whether his wife had received a support check he had mailed. The e-mail read simply: "Don't think I have it yet. It's been two weeks. Sure you sent it? If so, I'll keep looking." When Brian's coach phoned him to suggest gently that the e-mail seemed pretty innocuous to her, Brian flew into a rage. Even this mild reframe was too much for Brian. He accused his coach of being insensitive, partisan, unethical, and inept. He sent an e-mail to the entire team suggesting that his coach be replaced with someone more "supportive." After several conversations between Brian and his attorney, she was able to help Brian accept the fact that while he saw his coach as having let him down, the team did not. During these conversations, his attorney stuck to carefully paraphrasing Brian's comments, and empathizing with his need for support. She spent quite a bit of time simply listening quietly and acknowledging that the process was challenging. Ultimately, though, she stated in a clear but nonjudgmental tone that she believed Brian could work productively with his current coach, and that his coach genuinely wanted Brian to feel comfortable and successful in the process. Brian's attorney took the firm stance that she, and the team, could not support the replacement of Brian's coach, and gently advised him to move forward. Neither his attorney nor his coach (in a subsequent conversation) was able to help him recognize his distorted perceptions of both his wife's e-mail and his coach's response to it. All the professionals could do was provide him with supportive feedback, while setting ongoing and consistent limits on his subsequent behavior. Brian was able to continue in the Collaborative process and even to continue to work with his coach, but he remained brittle and hypersensitive. This was one of many such episodes.

Okay; now we have a framework for understanding whether a client has the inherent capacity for a transformative experience within the Collaborative process, or whether she is likely to scrape through by the skin of her teeth. We've learned that where Collaborative practice is concerned, one size definitely does not fit all. It is essential to understand where your client falls on the Rigidity/ Flexibility Continuum, and which techniques will work well for a client in that position, in order to intervene in effective ways.

I SAID I WANTED A COLLABORATIVE DIVORCE.
I NEVER SAID I DIDN'T WANT YOU TO SUFFER.

Before you throw up your hands and say "This is too complicated" or "I'm a lawyer, not a therapist. How am I supposed to make use of all this?" let's take a breath. First, much of this you already know intuitively. How many times have you said to your professional counterpart, "My client is really touchy about the very idea of spousal support. Let's find a way of talking about it that doesn't leave him feeling he's being taken advantage of"? Without knowing it, you've made some diagnostic assessments of your client and are putting them to work. Second, we don't expect you to understand your client from the outset. We advocate treating each case, from the beginning, as if it were transformative and, if necessary, adjust your expectations downward over time. Third, if

> "We advocate treating each case, from the beginning, as if it were transformative and, if necessary, adjust your expectations downward over time."

you are not a mental health professional, you can and should rely on the coaches on your team to educate you about the psychological makeup of your client and to strategize, along with you, about what techniques will work best for your case. If you all get stuck, you could even consider getting a consultation from a more experienced colleague.

▼▼▼▼▼

A Few Words on Splitting

The term "splitting" is bandied about quite a bit in Collaborative Practice, particularly by mental health professionals. Like so many clinical terms that have worked their way into colloquial use, this one can be confusing. We want to clarify that when we use the word "splitting" in a clinical or Collaborative context, we do not mean that someone or something is literally split off from something else (such as a rogue professional who begins to act on her own). In our context, the concept of splitting is psychological and refers to a powerful (and potentially toxic) defensive mechanism. We are talking about splitting here because rigid clients, like Brian in the above example, make heavy and persistent use of it.

Early in life we have the task of learning that the people who sometimes gratify us are the very same ones who sometimes disappoint us. If our parents and other caregivers are relatively responsive to us when we are young, then, over time, we can tolerate (even benefit from) their small lapses. For example, we can learn to live with the fact that Mom doesn't come every time we call, or that Dad won't always give us an extra cookie. We develop the capacity for ambivalence—the knowledge that trusted people love us even when they are not around, and that good and bad qualities can (and do!) coexist in the same person. Bad experience does not necessarily negate good.

We all utilize splitting from time to time. We are all vulnerable to forgetting that being let down by an important person doesn't make them an enemy. But if we are relatively healthy we can recover our sense of reality.

Some unfortunate people never develop the capacity to hold on to the idea that positive and negative attributes can exist in the same person. These are traumatized people whose ideas and behavior cluster at the rigid end of our Continuum. They live in a black-and-white world. For them, love is destroyed by hate, a feeling of support is destroyed by a feeling of being let down. So the only way to protect positive feelings about others is to keep them segregated from negative feelings. When a client experiences one member or members of the team as *on their side* (all good) and another member or members as *against them* (all bad), with no awareness of a middle ground, that's splitting at work.

Red Flags for Splitting

1. A client or professional sees the Collaborative landscape in black and white ("I'll either win or lose").

2. An idealized client or professional suddenly "falls off the pedestal" and becomes vilified.
3. A client reports that many people in her life have abandoned or betrayed her or reports a pattern of recurrent estrangement from friends and family.
4. A client takes an intense dislike to one or more professionals while adoring one or more of the others.
5. One or more members of the professional team find themselves intensely preferring one client over the other in a sustained way.

▼▼▼▼▼

Off the Continuum: The "Terrorist"

So now we've explored the ordinary range of "types" of clients that we work with in the Collaborative process—from those capable of some type of transformative experience to those for whom reaching agreement without litigation is a "good" outcome. But what about the outliers? If you've worked on several Collaborative cases and had the experience of some cases "falling out" of the process, you may have encountered what we have come to call The Terrorist.

The Terrorist is a client who has a tenuous engagement in the process from the beginning. Somewhere along the line (probably early on) you will realize that he has not "bought into" the Collaborative model. Instead, he seeks an abstract form of retribution for actual or perceived wrongs he has suffered at the hands of his spouse. He wants justice at all costs. He wants revenge. He wants to stand atop the mountain and shout to the masses: "See what she has done to me?" And he wants to hear the rallying cry "Yes, we hear you, you have been horribly wronged. You deserve compensation, and your spouse deserves to suffer."

The difference between the Terrorist and a client at the far rigid end of the Rigidity/Flexibility Continuum is that no amount of containment can bring a Terrorist into reality or help him or her to see reason. Where a highly rigid client, upon hearing that her husband had an affair, might very much want to punish him by going to court and suing him for all he is worth, she will probably be able to stay in the process—even if she never relinquishes her sense of herself as a martyr—simply because some part of her is operating in reality. In other words, though she may never be emotionally sated, her capacity to intellectually recognize that she will not get the emotional outcome she wants by litigating will likely be enough to keep her at the table.

The Terrorist, on the other hand, is not governed by reality. She is engaged in a holy war and the goal—to fulfill a moral quest—trumps rational thought. This is a client who is willing to risk it all in court, because to do anything else represents a capitulation to evil. If you have a client who is willing to act as a suicide bomber in the Collaborative process, there is nothing you can do to stop her.

▼▼▼▼▼

How Can I Know if a Case Is Right for Collaborative? Why Do Some Cases "Fall Out?"

It has been our happy experience that the vast majority of Collaborative cases reach a successful outcome, with both clients signing on to a final Agreement on financial and, if they have children, parenting issues. The authors' own anecdotal experience in our local metropolitan area of Washington, D.C., is that approximately 90 percent of our cases reach successful outcomes, while about 10 percent do not—and some of those in the 10 percent terminate quite early on in the process, usually within the first two or three meetings.

There has been writing and discussion in the Collaborative community about screening clients for Collaborative in order to increase chances for success and minimize the likelihood of setting clients up for an expensive, frustrating, and ultimately unsuccessful experience. From what we have read and been taught, the general wisdom seems to be that the only obvious disqualifiers are active domestic violence, untreated substance abuse, untreated mental illness, a history of chronic lying on the part of one or both spouses, or an incapacity of one or both spouses to recognize and acknowledge the other spouse's point of view. In practice, we have found that it is almost impossible to ascertain in advance which cases will be able to successfully reach a resolution. In fact, we have found that it is often the cases that look the easiest at the outset that prove the trickiest over time, and the cases that seem hopeless at first that result in the most satisfying successes.

In general, we like to err on the side of trying. Even clients with significant limitations may also have significant strengths that will allow them to progress with the help of a cohesive and skilled team. In addition, there are some factors that, while they may not move a couple toward a transformative experience, might keep the clients in the process long enough to reach Agreement. These factors include fear of a worse outcome in court and lack of financial resources to litigate. While we have never taken on a case that involves ongoing domestic violence, we have successfully participated in cases that have included serious substance abuse and characterological pathology.

> "... we have found that it is often the cases that look the easiest at the outset that prove the trickiest over time, and the cases that seem hopeless at first that result in the most satisfying successes. ... In general, we like to err on the side of trying."

When we are involved in a case that fails to reach successful resolution, we always ask ourselves, "Is there anything we could or should have done differently?" Because there are usually many complicated factors that become entwined in the toughest cases, this question will not have a simple answer. Still, exploring cases that go awry is an essential exercise. We've debriefed a number of unsuccessful cases, and here's what we have found: When one of our cases "falls out," it is because one client (or the couple) is too impaired to tolerate the model (e.g., "The Terrorist"), because one or more of the team professionals either hasn't yet learned to, or is unable to, function according to the principles of Collaborative Practice, or some combination of these factors. We have found that cases generally do *not* fall out over technical or procedural mistakes. Teams and clients recover from such errors if both the professionals and the clients are reasonably flexible and resilient.

APPLYING OUR UNDERSTANDING TO THE COLLABORATIVE PROCESS

THE COMPONENTS OF THE COLLABORATIVE PROCESS 5

Once we've completed our first Collaborative training, we have an idea of how a Collaborative case is conducted. Later, our practice group colleagues further influence our ideas about best practices. Other factors that help determine how we structure our cases are the availability of collaboratively trained professionals in the area in which we work and the financial resources of our clients. We authors have been open about our preference for the multidisciplinary team approach that follows Pauline Tesler and Peggy Thompson's model. Still, there is the ideal and there is the real. In practice, strict adherence to a prescribed method is not always in the best interests of a particular client.

At one time or another, we have found ourselves wondering if we could or should change the structure of the process in some way—take a shortcut, skip a step, blend steps into hybrids, work outside of the box—because we doubt that the ordinary structure will be effective for a *particular* client. Let's consider an example that often pops up early in the process.

Faced with impatient clients who voice concerns about looming costs, we may wonder if reading through the entire Collaborative Participation Agreement together at the first team meeting will be experienced by them as an expensive waste of time. We may ask ourselves: "Should we skip through the Agreement quickly and move on to interests and goals? The clients already understand the Agreement—we reviewed it when we first met." Experienced practitioners will likely respond, "No—we need to read through the Agreement thoroughly. I need to be sure my client understands all the clauses, and I am more comfortable following the structure as I was trained to do." In this example the more experienced practitioner probably wouldn't have much trouble selling his or her position to the team—if only on the basis of the need for full disclosure. But the need to "sell" best practice would be unnecessary if all the professionals on the team had a full grasp of why it is psychologically important to follow the structure.

As we've discussed, good parents have rules but don't stick to them arbitrarily. A clear set of parenting values and guidelines, applied to a growing understanding of their children's strengths, vulnerabilities, and needs, allows these parents to make thoughtful departures that don't destabilize themselves or their children. The same is true for us as Collaborative practitioners. If we stay tuned in to the question of "why ordinary Collaborative protocols work," and pair our understanding with an evolving sense of our clients' strengths, vulnerabilities, and needs, we will have the information we need to decide when to deviate (and when not to deviate) from ordinary practice. We want to dial up our collective awareness of the psychological impact of our procedural decisions.

This is a book about what is going on below the surface of Collaborative Practice. As we've written, we've grappled with the question of how much information to include about the concrete aspects (the "steps" and "protocols") of the process itself. We are going to review them here, but focus only briefly on the "what" and the "how" and emphasize the "why." As we review the familiar landmarks of our work, we will be asking such questions as "Why does this work?" and "Why is this important?" The answers to these questions provide compass points for our work from start to finish.

Now we'll walk you through the Collaborative process (as it is described by Tesler and Thompson, as taught by major training groups, and as set out by the International Academy of Collaborative Professionals) from a psychological perspective. We assume our readers have a fundamental familiarity with this structure; by exploring it from the inside out, we hope to deepen your understanding and give you tools to navigate more easily.

FIRST INDIVIDUAL MEETING WITH A CLIENT

We will start with a look at a meeting with a client who has already chosen Collaborative as his dispute resolution model, and has "buy in" from his partner or spouse. We are assuming that the client has already been educated about other process options (including mediation and litigation), and has been informed of the advantages and disadvantages of each. Our client has perhaps already retained a Collaborative team and is now meeting with you (his attorney, mental health professional, or financial neutral).

If we were to think about agenda items or goals for this conversation, they might look something like this:

- Begin to establish the Microcontainer and a working alliance (by listening to the client's story, establishing an emotional connection, creating a sense of safety, etc.).
- Help the client to develop a sense of you as the professional.
- Get your first sense of where the client falls on the Rigidity/ Flexibility Continuum.
- Educate the client about some of the nuts and bolts of the Collaborative process—particularly issues of confidentiality, privileged communication, full disclosure, and transparency.

We will make our decisions about sequencing and emphasis based on how our client presents as he walks in the door and how much he already knows about how Collaborative works. But no matter how you structure the components of this conversation, remember: *everything has meaning.*

EVERYTHING HAS MEANING

From the moment you shake your new client's hand, you should begin to form hypotheses about how this person functions, how he thinks, and what he is likely to need from you in order to move through the process successfully. Notice everything. Pay attention to your reactions to your client from the start. Does your client walk in and admire your artwork? Does he ask for coffee?

> "As soon as you shake your new client's hand, you should begin to form hypotheses about how this person functions, how he thinks, and what he will need from you in order to move through the process successfully."

Does he plop down on the couch, heave a long sigh, and look at you expectantly? The aspects of his character contained in these leading presentations are data points that can help you begin to paint a psychological portrait of your client.

YOUR CLIENT'S STORY

Try to listen to your client's story with a fresh ear. Rather than relying on the professional experience you have accumulated as a shorthand to understanding (after all, we do come to recognize certain "types" and scenarios over time), try to keep your mind open to this client as being unique in the way he feels, perceives, experiences, and interprets his world. Your initial discussion will likely cover a wide range of topics, including a narrative about his spouse and their marriage, how the decision to separate or divorce was reached, some information about their children, and aspects of their professional and financial status. You will want to hear the story as your client recalls and organizes it, and learn about the cast of characters and the roles your client feels each person has played. You will be listening for important moments, turning points, or meaningful events that stand out for your client and may carry specific weight in the process to come.

You will listen for some crucial information about how this person thinks. Is the story well organized (with a sequence of events we can follow), or does it jump from past to present and back again with such rapidity that you have a hard time following the flow?

You will want to know if this person describes people—particularly his spouse—in shades of gray (including both strengths and weaknesses) or if he sees others in black and white (all bad or all good). An important question is: does

> ▼
>
> "We are listening for important moments, turning points, or meaningful events that stand out for our client and may carry specific weight during the process to come."

your client perceive his spouse as a good parent (even if she had failings as a wife), or does he see her as an unfit mother as well as an unfaithful spouse? The answer to this question is crucial, as it gives us early clues as to whether or not your client and the Collaborative process are a natural fit. As we discussed previously, if your client tells his story without self-reflection, without owning any piece of the marital problems, and without some significant areas of empathy and respect for his spouse, the likelihood of working effectively with the client in a Collaborative process will be diminished.

EXPLAINING THE PROCESS MORE FULLY

At some point during this meeting, you likely want to briefly describe the "flow" of the Collaborative process. You will want to help your client to anticipate a series of meetings with the attorneys to work on financial matters, and, if the couple has children, a series of meetings to construct the parenting plan (with coaches if there are coaches on the team, or with the attorneys if there aren't). We tend not to spend a lot of time describing the role of the neutrals in this very first meeting (in recognition of the fact that our clients may already feel overwhelmed with information), but we lay the groundwork by suggesting that we may choose to call on neutral collaboratively trained experts in both child-related and financial issues to help the team and the clients develop the best possible plans for their future.

We also describe the open communication that flows between team members, and we note that we will have conference calls with the other professionals on a regular basis to address clients' concerns, plan for meetings, and decide how best to move the process along. Many of these nuts and bolts will be reviewed again

▼

"Education is, of course, an ethical necessity; we need our clients to know what they are signing on for. But it also helps anxious clients to begin to relax and to move into a mode of rational thinking."

during the first team meeting, but the repetition will be helpful in clarifying what can be a confusing process for new clients. Education is, of course, an ethical necessity; we need our clients to know what they are signing on for. But it also helps anxious clients to begin to relax and to move into a mode of rational thinking. Clients who come to their first meeting with us in an understandably heightened emotional state are often calmed when they are given a road map of *what to expect.*

▼▼▼▼▼

Client Traits to Attend to in the First Meeting(s)

Cognitive Style

Intellectual capacity
Organization of thinking—coherence, sequencing, logic
Capacity for abstract thinking versus concrete thinking

Insight—Self-Reflection

Capacity for honest sharing
Awareness of own flaws, mistakes
Awareness of own emotions
Empathy for spouse, children, others
Nuanced understanding of marital relationship and its
    dissolution
Ability to see others and life situations in "shades of gray"
    versus "black and white"

Emotional Style

Intensity of emotional state
Mode of expression of emotion (does the presentation match
    the feeling?)

Contained versus overwhelmed

Guarded/defensive versus open/vulnerable

Grieving/angry versus raging/vengeful

Capacity for self-regulation (capacity to recover when emotionally destabilized) versus wildly fluctuating intense emotional states

Interpersonal Style

Level of social skill and attunement to others

Capacity to carry on reciprocal conversation with shared talking and listening

Assertiveness versus passivity

"Likability"—warmth, friendliness, sense of humor, capacity to be pleasant

Eccentricities or oddness

Wish to see you as a competent professional versus distrust or devaluing of you

General Mental Health

Presentation or report of symptoms

Mood

Capacity for rational thought

Level of suspiciousness/paranoia

Presentation or report of substance abuse

Presentation or report of domestic violence or abuse

HOT SPOTS AND COPING STRATEGIES

In this and other early meetings, we like to look for opportunities to help our clients to identify some of their emotional "hot spots" and to begin to help them learn to expect and manage emotional

▼

"If our client tells his story without self-reflection, without owning any piece of the marital problems, and without some significant areas of empathy and respect for his spouse, the likelihood of working effectively with the client in a Collaborative process is diminished."

flare-ups. As an example, a client might tell you: "If the team can just get my wife to stop yelling at me, I will feel this process is a success!" You might respond: "When you mentioned how nice it would be if your wife stopped yelling at you, I wondered if her yelling might be a real trigger for you—does she sort of push your buttons when she yells? Does that make it hard for you to listen or respond in a calm way?" This exchange will be the springboard for a useful conversation with your new client. You will already be beginning to help him to anticipate a way in which his marital dynamic will likely play out in the Collaborative process, as well as the reactions this dynamic will provoke in him. You will then be on your way toward helping him to develop new coping strategies and more productive responses.

▼▼▼▼▼

Examples of Coping Strategies We Might Teach Our Clients

Coping strategies during meetings:
- Taking a few minutes in advance of a team meeting to confer with their coach and/or attorney in order to anticipate and emotionally prepare for likely triggers
- Asking for a break from a meeting to confer with their attorney and/or coach
- Writing some statements in advance of a meeting that can be read during the meeting when strong emotions are triggered

Coping strategies for use between meetings:
- Setting limits on difficult or provocative conversations with a spouse by ending them firmly but politely
- Taking a "time out" and spending time alone, reminding oneself (and one's spouse) that a given issue "belongs" in the Collaborative process

BEGINNING TO DEVELOP A COLLABORATIVE ALLIANCE WITH YOUR CLIENT

Throughout this first meeting, there is an underlying emotional flow, a connection that develops with varying levels of intensity for different professional/client pairs. The special relationship that begins in this first meeting and builds over time we call the "Collaborative alliance." The Collaborative alliance differs from a therapeutic alliance in that it is *more* goal specific, and from an ordinary attorney/client relationship or financial professional/ client relationship in that it is *less* goal specific. The Collaborative alliance is designed to support both the individual client and the entire family in emerging from the divorce process spiritually, psychologically, and financially intact. The strength of the Collaborative alliance will depend on the amount of overlap between the professional's conceptualization of the Collaborative process and the client's. Depending on where your clients fall on the Rigidity/ Flexibility Continuum and on what circumstances have brought them into the process, they will be more or less likely to embrace the higher-level goal of protecting and promoting the needs of everyone in the family (including their spouse). In fact, one of the most common red flags at the start of a Collaborative case is a difficulty in developing a shared sense of purpose with your client. If you finish your first meeting with your new Collaborative client frustrated by your failure to connect, you may be facing a fundamental inability in your client to imagine the possibility of your being able simultaneously to support his interests *and* those of his entire family.

▼▼▼▼▼

Building a Collaborative Alliance

- Try to "walk a mile in the shoes of your client" (develop empathy).
- Convey empathy and compassion, but avoid saying anything negative about your client's spouse (there is a big

difference between saying "It sounds like you feel she hasn't been much of a mother" and "Your wife hasn't been much of a mother, has she?").

- Acknowledge your client's feelings and views but also occasionally wonder aloud about the other client's feelings and views ("Sounds like you think she hasn't been much of a mother. Any thoughts about how she would characterize you as a parent?").

- Convey to your client that you are on his side—but you are not "against" the other client, and your goal and wish is to be helpful to the client in a manner that is supportive of a good outcome for the entire family ("I get it—you'd very much like to stay in the house. We'll keep that wish of yours in mind as we move through this process and explore your needs, your wife's needs, your kids' needs, and what might be possible.").

You should consider yourself successful in beginning to build a Collaborative alliance if your client leaves your first meeting or meetings feeling listened to closely and compassionately, trusting that you have begun to understand his views and needs, and believing you to be knowledgeable and skilled in your role as his guide. If you have given your client a clearer vision of the journey ahead and have already begun preparing him for rough patches in the road, he will be relieved to have found you. Your case will be off to a solid beginning.

THE FIRST TEAM CONVERSATION PRIOR TO A TEAM MEETING: COMING TOGETHER AS A TEAM

One of the best decisions a team can make when starting a case is to organize a team conference call or meeting prior to bringing the clients to the first team meeting. This conversation helps begin to establish team cohesion and set the structure of the process for that particular team.

The recently published the book *The Checklist Manifesto* by Atul Gawande prompted us to think more about the role of careful team preparation. The author makes the point that when professional work is intellectually complex, errors tend to be related to lapses in procedure rather than failures of expertise. In other words, the more we know about what we do, the more likely it is that when we make mistakes they could have been avoided. His thesis is that the simple checklist, something we often use early in our careers and let go of as we gain experience, is critical to avoiding mistakes in every field.

Experience has shown us that the more emotionally fraught a Collaborative case is, the greater the likelihood that team members will make errors or omissions in procedure. These errors, in turn, will reinforce the emotional challenges in the case. Reviewing a team checklist at the start of a case does not mean that agreed-upon protocols will not later be bent or broken. But it does give your team the best shot at smooth going, and it does provide a set of shared expectations to which you can refer back when the going gets rough.

CHECKLIST FOR FIRST TEAM PROFESSIONALS' CONVERSATION*

❏ Assign a note taker.
❏ Obtain contact information, preferred e-mail address, and telephone numbers for each team member.
❏ Discuss how each professional views his/her role.
❏ Discuss how each professional views working as a team.
❏ Discuss team members' views of who drives process decisions, the team or the clients?
❏ Discuss the coaches' role:
    ❏ How do team members view coaches' role in meetings?
    ❏ How do team members view the coaches' role vis-à-vis other team members?
    ❏ How does each coach view her/his role with the client and in the process?

---

* We are grateful to our colleagues in the D.C. Metro Protocols Committee for sharing this checklist with us.

❏ Discuss Meetings:
  ❏ Location
  ❏ Length
  ❏ Scheduling—consider scheduling full team/client meetings in advance
  ❏ Who should attend
  ❏ Breaks during the meeting
  ❏ Check-ins before the meeting: team members with clients and with each other
  ❏ Debriefing after the meeting: coaches and attorneys debrief with each client and team members debrief together
❏ Discuss and agree on a plan for ongoing team communications
  ❏ Weekly conference calls and what mechanism will be used for the conference calls, who will facilitate the calls
  ❏ E-mails—frequency, subject line (best to include the case name and note specifically when an e-mail is for the "TEAM ONLY"), billing, team meetings
  ❏ Communications with the team after professionals' meetings with clients
  ❏ Billing time for team communications
  ❏ What will be communicated to the clients about team communications?
  ❏ Discuss how/when each team member would like feedback about their work from other team members
❏ Discuss what each team member learned in their first conversations with their client
❏ Discuss in what order clients shall meet with professionals
❏ Discuss potential configurations of meetings (which professionals will attend which meetings)
❏ Discuss confidentiality and flow of communication within the team (including privilege of attorney/client and limits of privilege for coach/client)
❏ Set dates for potential team meetings with clients
❏ Discuss seating arrangements for team meetings with clients
❏ Discuss who will facilitate team meetings with clients

❑ Discuss who will write on the flip chart for team meetings with clients

❑ Discuss whether any team members or clients will caucus separately during team meetings with clients and whether team members will break to meet on their own

❑ Share information about what issues/topics are difficult for the clients and how to assist them in working through those issues/topics

❑ Share engagement agreements and Collaborative contracts

❑ Discuss rates, each professional's expectation regarding prompt payment of accounts receivable, and any billing rate variances that might create difficulties in the Collaborative process

❑ Discuss what each professional charges for team meetings, and phone calls, email review, travel, etc.

▼▼▼▼▼

Giving and Receiving Feedback

Many of us have struggled with the issue of how and when to give and get feedback about our work—whether positive or negative—within the Collaborative process. We suggest that during your initial team conversation you and your team address this issue head on. Ask each other: "How would you like to receive feedback? In what setting? In what form?" Some colleagues might prefer a conversation in person with their team. Others might feel more comfortable receiving an e-mail "heads up" prior to any feedback conversation so they can process the comments privately before facing their team. In any case, simply acknowledging that such give-and-take is a normal and necessary part of our work can help set the stage for the successful working through of any problems that may crop up as the process unfolds.

THE FIRST TEAM MEETING AND SIGNING
OF THE PARTICIPATION AGREEMENT

Clients come to the first team meeting almost universally tense and anxious. They have to face their spouse—sometimes after a prolonged period of acrimony, sometimes having had no contact for a period of time. They are about to meet their spouse's lawyer—who, at the start of the process, may still seem like a fearsome adversary. In a full team model, the clients are also about to meet their spouse's coach, a figure their spouse has already confided in privately. Some clients worry that their spouse's coach will judge them harshly or be angry with them on behalf of their spouse.

The primary emotional benefit of the first meeting is that clients can learn from it that all the team professionals are caring people who carry no judgment about either of them. If the professionals are able to convey authentic interest in the welfare of *both* clients as the meeting progresses, the clients will relax significantly and experience the Collaborative team as potentially helpful and supportive as a unit. Frightening fantasies can be replaced with real information about actual people.

> "The primary emotional benefit of the first meeting is that clients can learn from it that the team professionals are caring people who bring no judgment about either of them. . . . Frightening fantasies can be replaced with real information about actual people."

The clients' perception of the professionals as a cohesive team is consolidated as the meeting progresses by both the meeting's content and its process. Some teams opt to have the attorneys take turns reading through the clauses of the Participation Agreement, while other teams prefer that all professionals take a turn. Some teams even ask the clients to participate in the reading. We don't have a particular preference, but we do think that professionals (coaches, financial neutrals, child specialists) who are not participating in the actual reading (or oral summary) of the document should listen actively, appear interested, and, when appropriate, offer explicative comments. When every professional remains engaged and participatory, clients receive the message that the group is non-hierarchical—everyone at the table is a peer, and everyone is committed to working together from start to finish. Further, moving systematically through the Agreement conveys to the clients that their entire team understands the Agreement and takes it very seriously; everyone supports the principles and guidelines it contains.

Throughout the first meeting, more subtle positive and negative messages may be conveyed to clients by the nonverbal behaviors and off-topic, informal conversations that occur between professionals. In Chapter 3 we went into detail about the risks of too much banter between professionals during any Collaborative meeting. Here we want to highlight that clients will likely be set at ease by what they perceive to be a friendly and mutually respectful, but professionally appropriate, rapport among members of their team.

On the other hand, we recognize that some clients—particularly those who have more intense mistrust of or hostility toward their spouse—may experience the cooperative atmosphere in the first meeting as unsettling. For these clients, the idea that their attorney and coach are not "against" the other spouse (quite the contrary!) may raise their anxiety and undercut their trust in their own team professionals. Even though every client who chooses Collaborative divorce has been educated about its philosophy, seeing that philosophy in action at the first meeting can be difficult for some. One of our colleagues describes a vignette that beautifully illustrates the way in which our clients observe our professional interactions, sometimes reacting in unpredictable ways:

Before we got started at the signing meeting, I remembered that I had a book belonging to the other attorney. I mentioned to her that I wanted to return the book to her while we were together that day. During a break in the middle of the meeting, I stepped into my office, grabbed the book, and handed it back to my colleague as we reconvened at the conference room table. I thanked her for lending it to me, and she thanked me for returning it. When I debriefed with my client after the meeting, he noted with concern that I was clearly friendly with his wife's attorney to a degree he had not anticipated.

I recalled that when he and I had met for the first time and he had mentioned to me the name of the attorney his wife had retained, I had told him I thought she was a great attorney, a good collaborator, and a really decent person. She was not, in fact, a friend of mine, and I didn't describe her as one. So when my client saw our book exchange, he suddenly felt suspicious that I had not fully explained my relationship with the attorney on the other side, and he worried that, given our friendliness, I might not "advocate strenuously" on his behalf. This was actually a very useful red flag and wake-up call for me. I realized the depth of his worry about the Collaborative model, I realized the challenge he was facing in developing a sturdy trust in me, and I realized that the team and I would need to stay tuned in to how these clients felt about the way we work with each other. It made me remember that not all clients feel comfortable with the notion that in Collaborative Practice, attorneys work together, and the team effectiveness rests on solid and friendly relationships with one another rather than on adversarial strategizing against one another.—Maryland Attorney

Whether clients find our collegiality reassuring or worrisome offers one important piece of helpful psychological information about them. As we move into talking about goals and interests, we will be able to learn more. How do our clients interact nonverbally while articulating their thoughts and feelings? For example, we may observe that the husband tends to sit back quietly while his wife speaks for both of them, and that he has difficulty expressing his own feelings. We might learn that the wife feels so worried about achieving financial security in her future that she begins to weep whenever she talks about money—and that her tears provoke immediate irritation in her husband (who sees her tears as manipulative). The very process of eliciting goals offers a wealth of information. Is one or both of our clients able to distinguish between goals and interests? If not, are they simply confused or are their characters organized in such a way that they are unable to think beyond their own specific desires? So, for example, can "My goal is to stay in the house" be transformed (with our help) into "My interest is for each of us to live in a comfortable place where our children can feel safe and well taken care of"? If our client is able to distinguish between goals and interests, is she impatient with the process of generating global goals and interests, or does she see the intrinsic value of this phase of the process? Has she done some internal preparatory work, or is she thinking about these concepts now, for the first time? Or, as we sometimes see, has she come to the meeting with a carefully prepared outline of goals and subgoals?

In this first meeting, we might hear that our clients share most goals and interests and feel supportive of one another, or that they have conflicting goals and find that fact frightening, or angering, or surprising—all extremely helpful information for each professional at the table to file away and draw on over time in their efforts to help their clients work effectively together to reach resolutions.

The discussion about client goals and interests gives our clients a preview of how future meetings will be conducted and how the clients themselves might feel during those meetings. As the team professionals "check in" with each client, both clients will begin to experience the team's interest in and concern for them. By observing our behavior toward them and toward our team members, clients will also get their first taste of the fundamental expectation by the team that they will share air time, listen to one another, and behave respectfully.

When an initial meeting is difficult or fraught, the reactions of each team professional are powerfully affecting for our clients. Clients notice if one attorney responds empathically while the other remains silent. They notice if their coach is helpful or passively observant. While clients may take in and retain little of what is actually *said* during this meeting, they will take away a powerful set of visceral reactions.

If the meeting goes relatively well (with all team professionals successfully conveying nonjudgmental interest and concern for both clients, and with both clients feeling they had an equal opportunity to speak and be heard), then it will offer a helpful foundation for the process to come. On the other hand, if clients feel that something unfair has occurred or something insensitive has been said, they may feel that amends should be made. One of the challenges of Collaborative Practice is that the fact that a client wants something from one of us (an apology, a retraction, more

> ▼
>
> "Clients notice if one attorney responds empathically while the other remains silent. They notice if their coach is helpful or passively observant. While they may take in little of what is actually said, they will take away a powerful set of visceral reactions."

support) does not mean that we should offer it. We don't want to be reflexively dismissive—sometimes our clients have legitimate complaints about us, and we should own our failures. But as we've been discussing, our clients' negative subjective experience is not always based on an accurate "read" of us or the group process; sometimes a complaint is a symptom of the client's own transference and distorted perception.

This first meeting is our clients' initial experience of the Macrocontainer. The more cohesive the team, the stronger and more reliable the container (and process) will feel. In Chapter 6 we will discuss in detail the various ways in which teams might fail to function cohesively, thus failing to establish a sturdy Macrocontainer. Here we'll simply say that if the clients sense rivalry, dislike, or mistrust between any of the team professionals, the container will be, and feel, fragile and unreliable. This lack of integrity in the container will leave the clients feeling mistrustful, discouraged, and frightened. We are aiming to establish a sturdy Macrocontainer, one that allows clients to leave the first meeting feeling that this group of professionals really cares about their family and can really help.

BRAINSTORMING, OPTION DEVELOPMENT, AND OPTION EVALUATION

When Collaborative professionals think about which core concepts and techniques make the Collaborative process "collaborative," we generally turn to the heart of interest-based negotiation and the techniques of brainstorming, option development, and the later evaluation of options. Techniques developed within the mediation field in large part by the Harvard Negotiation Project (*Getting to Yes*, by Roger Fisher and Bruce Patton) are familiar and they form the foundation of our Collaborative skills repertoire and of the way we structure meetings. Again, what we would like to do here is take our readers beneath the surface of the explicit utility and function of these techniques in order to explore the emotional payoff that these tools deliver to our clients and to our process.

While there is an important place in Collaborative Practice for rational, logical, and analytical thinking, success relies on our capacity to work "out of the box." Additionally, durable agreements are durable because they have taken emotion into account as they were developed. When you invite your client to brainstorm ideas freely, without concern for actual or potential obstacles or her spouse's (or team's) imagined negative reactions, you are helping her to access her creativity, her fantasies, her wishes, and her hopes. The process of brainstorming accesses the right brain (the emotionally driven part). As our clients' guides, we want to create an environment that allows for openness of mind.

Brainstorming is critical for another reason. When we reassure the clients that there is an importance to generating ideas without evaluation, and when we support the spouses who are listening and tolerating the introduction of options that they may experience as ridiculous, threat-

> "When you invite your client to brainstorm ideas freely, without concern for actual or potential obstacles or her spouse's (or team's) imagined negative reactions, you are helping her to access her creativity, her fantasies, her wishes, and her hopes."

ening, or hurtful, we are laying the foundation for a potentially transformative experience. For many of our clients, our belief in the possibility of bringing together what first appear as hopelessly competing interests into an integrated whole is a revelation.

In all the behaviors we employ as team professionals during each Collaborative meeting—especially when option development is part of the discussion—we are employing the best kind of parenting models. Remember the good mother in Chapter 1? She is able to create a safe psychological environment through 1) her capacity to recognize and tolerate her child's states of anxiety and distress and to contain those states without retaliating, withdrawing, or moving too fast to action, 2) her willingness to entertain the idea that there might be multiple sources of the distress, and 3) her communication of her understanding of her child. This environment is one in which the child can develop a sense of himself and the world as one in which discomfort and confusion—both physical and emotional—can be tolerated, understood, metabolized, and resolved without destruction or harm to himself or his mother.

As we guide our clients through option generation and option evaluation, the team, like the good parent, is modeling the capacity to tolerate powerful and often conflicting ideas and feelings from their clients without becoming anxious, angry, or positional. By working together as a team in an ongoing dialogue about the clients and by gently insisting that the clients make their own decisions, we are modeling the healthy parent's focused attention on his or her child and belief in that child's developmental capacities. When a team is working well together (again, we will say more about this in Chapter 6), all professionals are tuned in to the clients' needs and the process on all levels. When we bring our entire selves to bear—emotional understanding, cognitive analysis, physical energy, and enthusiasm—we are creating a unique emotional environment in which affects can be tolerated and worked through without derailing the actual Collaborative work, and both individual and family development can be fostered.

> ▼
>
> "As we guide our clients through option generation and option evaluation, the team, like the good mother, is modeling the capacity to tolerate powerful and often conflicting ideas and feelings from their clients without becoming anxious, angry, or positional."

THE FLIP CHART

As we all know, the flip chart is the ubiquitous tool of Collaborative practitioners. It is even an emblem of our work, showing up on the cover of brochures and in website pictures of Collaborative meetings. In this age of rapidly developing technology, some practitioners have replaced the traditional paper and easel with an electronic wall screen on which they project notes as they are typed into a computer. We want to talk briefly about the flip chart, both the traditional model and the high-tech version.

The flip chart's explicit purpose is to help keep the team and the clients organized. At the outset of each meeting, we use it to:

- Record agenda items.
- Record estimated time frames for each piece of the discussion in order to keep the group on track.
- Record reminders about homework to be done as the discussion progresses.
- List "parking lot" issues on which we intend to focus during a subsequent meeting.
- Log the options generated by the clients during brainstorm sessions.
- Keep track of clients' reactions to options (sometimes writing a "yes," "no," or "maybe" next to each option in order to find areas of overlap).

Most interesting, though, are the ways in which the lowly flip chart supports, maintains, and facilitates the essential emotional and cognitive processes of a Collaborative meeting. As the discussion proceeds and options are generated (along with powerful emotions), the flip chart becomes the tangible, visible representation of a psychological space in which ideas and feelings—sometimes competing, often powerfully charged—can coexist and be tolerated. The words on the page, though they represent all the complexities and challenges faced by the team, can remain fixed, can be manipulated in space (sentences can be moved or removed, arrows and circles can be drawn, etc.), but no actual action is immediately required. The flip chart, which can be easily viewed by both the clients and the team, communicates the message: "All of us over here (including both clients) are on the same team; over there, on that flip chart, are the goals and hopes of this team for resolution and a satisfactory result of this process. It and we are all we need to get us where we need to go."

Additionally, the flip chart symbolizes the continuity of work that the Collaborative team is engaged in. Our clients are naturally buffeted about during the emotional storm that is any divorce, and their states of mind shift from meeting to meeting. It can be difficult for them to hold options or agreements in mind from meeting to meeting, or to remember the ways in which their own ideas developed. Flip chart notes exist and are carried over unaltered from meeting to meeting, memorializing ideas and recording the narrative of a case as it develops. The flip chart represents a group mind, a sturdy container—the notion that even when emotions are high,

> "The flip chart represents a group mind, a sturdy container—the notion that even when emotions are high, the team can retain the capacity to think."

the team can retain the capacity to think. We can hold onto ideas, safe in our assurance that they don't hold us captive but rather represent our capacity to massage them, over time, into a shape that both clients can feel good about.

Our recording of the history, or story, of a case over various phases of its development depicts an evolution from, rather than an annihilation of, earlier experience. A painful aspect of many divorcing couples' communication is the repeated and circular fighting that occurs about what actually *happened* in their marriage, and a hopelessness each partner often feels about ever having his or her memory or perception confirmed. We review old flip chart notes in order to clarify differences in recall and, without judgment or criticism, establish what was said or done previously *in order to proceed most effectively rather than to determine who was right or wrong*. Our flip chart records the emotional progress that a couple makes away from a preoccupation with the past toward a focus on the future.

▼▼▼▼▼

Summary of the Functions of the Flip Chart

- Helps the team to organize complex ideas so that meetings can run smoothly.
- Symbolizes a psychological space in which competing ideas can be tolerated and reconciled.

- Draws emotional energy from the table and organizes it into a point of common focus.
- Represents the continuity of ideas.
- Depicts and furthers our clients' emotional development and movement toward resolution.

A Few Words on the Use of the "Parking Lot"

When an issue comes up that, while important, is not immediately relevant or could derail the process, team members often write it in their notes or on the flip chart in an imaginary space called the "parking lot." While doing this, we often tell our clients something like: "That's an important question. We can't really answer it right now, so let's put it in the parking lot. If we don't get to it naturally, let's be sure to decide, before we leave today, when we will get to it." In this simple way, we are again modeling good parental behavior. We are conveying the following set of messages: "We hear your concern, we acknowledge its importance, we can hold it in mind without moving too quickly to action, we trust that you can bear delaying immediate gratification, and you can trust that this process will address your concerns at some point in the future."

THE MISSION STATEMENT

The Mission Statement, whether it is a prose narrative or a series of "bullet points," records our clients' goals for their Collaborative process. We can help clients work on such a statement in any early meeting at which both clients are present. Some teams choose to make the development of the Mission Statement a task of the first team meeting in which the clients sign the Participation Agreement and review goals and interests; other teams choose the first attorneys' or coaches' meeting. Because the moment in which the

Mission Statement is constructed is such a powerfully important moment in the beginning of a case, we suggest that whenever possible all team members be present at the table.

The Mission Statement is constructed from the list of goals and interests that the clients spontaneously articulate, and from their responses to our question "Why did you each choose Collaborative as a model, rather than some other process?" Goals are generally explicit and often reference concrete objects of desire ("I want to be able to buy a house once this process is over"). Interests include emotional needs for the self, for the children, or for the family, and often drive goals. Sometimes clients are easily able to articulate interests; other times they need our help in unpacking goals to reach interests. When a client moves from "I must stay in the marital home" to "I want my children to feel good spending time with me," they have moved from a goal to an interest.

As with everything else we observe in our clients, the construction of the Mission Statement is a rich assessment tool. This is another opportunity for us to observe the way our clients relate to us, each other, and the task. Do they find the construction of the Mission Statement a relieving opportunity to voice what has been on their mind, or do they have trouble accessing or articulating goals and interests? Do they actively participate? Do they hold back? Does one dominate while the other remains passive? Do they focus on their children, or fail to mention them? How much overlap is there between one client's goals and interests and the other's? Do they use this moment as an opportunity to attack each other, or as a joining experience? By contrast, is there a superficial Pollyanna approach to the task that skips over what realistically will be tough work ("I want us to keep doing all the fun things we do as a family now—we want to stay close, and be good friends.")? As we have said before, everything has meaning. So in addition to paying close attention to the content of the Mission Statement as it evolves, stay tuned in to the process of its creation.

Some Collaborative professionals keep the Mission Statement front and center as their work progresses. Many include the Mission Statement as a heading for every set of minutes they circulate; and others like to hold on to the flip chart pages that capture the Statement and post them on the wall at each meeting. When option evaluation becomes acrimonious, when clients lose their sense of commitment to the process, or when the team reaches impasse, the Mission Statement can become a North Star—a navigational tool that re-centers the team and gets them back on course.

"When option evaluation becomes acrimonious, when clients lose their sense of commitment to the process, or when the team reaches impasse, the mission statement can become a North Star—a navigational tool that re-centers the team and gets them back on course."

ANCILLARY CLIENT MEETINGS AND CONTACT THROUGHOUT THE PROCESS

Throughout every case, we all stay in touch with our clients—to varying degrees and in varying ways. We check in with clients on the phone, exchange e-mails, and meet with them individually and in various subgroups of professionals and client. A coach and an attorney might meet with their common client together; the financial neutral might meet with one client along with his coach. A range of meeting configurations is available to us, and, as we move through a case, we choreograph our dance according to an unfolding understanding of what makes sense.

Many of these contacts are brief and are focused on offering a quick injection of support to the client, answering a quick question, or obtaining a quick piece of information from the client that we need to help update the team. Other contacts require greater thoughtfulness and planning. Meetings of import relating to an issue that is immediately relevant to the process (these meetings are usually face-to-face) should be either disclosed to and discussed with the rest of the team or a planned outcome of a team discussion.

The fundamental function of ancillary contacts and meetings is to nurture and strengthen our relationships with our clients. With each contact, we gain a deeper understanding of our clients and they gain a clearer sense of us. When we are proactively in contact with our clients when we sense a need, and are responsive when they ask for contact, we further their trust in us. When misunderstandings develop between clients and team members, when our Collaborative alliance is shaken, these contacts allow us opportunities to reestablish trust. We have found that our clients' needs for ancillary contact stretches out on a long continuum from very low—which we may understand as avoidance—to very high—which we may understand as dependence, high anxiety, and/or enacting of transference. As we make decisions about how often and quickly to offer ancillary contact to our individual clients, we must balance our desire to offer adequate emotional support with necessary limit setting.

EMOTIONAL CONTAINMENT AND E-MAIL COMMUNICATION

As with ancillary meetings and telephone contact, there is great variability in the way clients approach e-mail usage. Some clients—even those still living in the same house with their spouse—e-mail one another frequently and imbue their missives with emotional and provocative messages. Some clients frequently forward these e-mails to their team verbatim as evidence of what they "go through" or for help setting limits. Others e-mail their team members frequently for help managing their own emotional states or for answers to practical questions. Some client e-mails are brief; others are long, rambling, and ruminative. When you perceive that e-mail communication is of significant frequency or emotional intensity, that's your cue that your client is struggling with the management of his internal state.

> "A client who is a 'high-intensity e-mailer' is offering you a window on the intensity of his emotions. He wants you to acknowledge and respond to his experience; he wants to draw you in. [He] will need thoughtful and sensitively timed feedback and guidance from his Collaborative team in order to help him remain helpfully engaged."

A client who is a "high-intensity e-mailer" is offering you a window on the intensity of his emotions. He wants you to acknowledge and respond to his experience; he wants to draw you in. If he is a more rigid client, he wants to offer written evidence that you should consider his perspective the only valid perspective, and a desire for you to join him in vilifying his spouse. This client will need thoughtful and sensitively timed feedback and guidance from his Collaborative team in order to help him remain helpfully engaged.

Some highly emotional and needy clients are best served when we provide guidelines for communication between them and their spouse. We might suggest they limit their e-mail communication in frequency (e.g., to once a day, or each time the children transition), that they limit their e-mails in length (e.g., keeping them to no more than three bullet points per message), and/or that they limit the content of their e-mails to logistical issues only (e.g., requested changes in schedule).

For clients who have been communicating with one another with particular hostility and who exhibit particularly enmeshed patterns of relating, we might also consider asking our clients to copy us on their e-mails, with the understanding that if they are unable to follow the guidelines upon which we have agreed, we will step in. For clients who acknowledge difficulty crafting e-mails that are "business only" (easily slipping into emotional rants or accusations), we might offer to read and suggest helpful "edits" for e-mails before they send them. In this way, we begin to act not only as their professional advisor, but also as a sort of external observing ego. We stand by, ready and able to help them regain their balance or rationality when it is eclipsed by old emotional dynamics. It is our hope that, over time, our clients will internalize our repeated guidance, our "voice," so that they can begin to self-correct without our real-time support.

In addition to monitoring clients' e-mails, we have also occasionally decided not to send them minutes of each meeting by e-mail in favor of reviewing them in person at the start of the next meeting. This technique has been helpful in the rare cases in which even the minutes or summaries of a meeting can trigger powerful negative reactions in either client, which might then be explosively expressed in e-mail exchanges between Collaborative meetings.

Many clients need and benefit from a rhythmic and reliable pattern of communication with us. We might suggest that we have a phone conversation the night before each team meeting and/or meet for an individual session just prior to each team meeting. In general, when we are working with an emotionally overwhelmed client, we want to offer more opportunity to talk things through with us. We want to offer soothing reassurance and encouragement to use their adult, mature, and thinking self. We want to repeatedly remind them of the tasks they want to accomplish. When necessary, we direct their thinking back to their goals and interests, to their Mission Statement, to their love of their children—whatever anchors will help ground them when they feel flooded by emotion.

At the same time, we don't want to unintentionally encourage our client to indulge in black-and-white thinking or become entrenched in rigid positions. Venting for venting's sake is generally unproductive, and providing too much opportunity for an angry client to delve more deeply into the reasons for his anger can often fuel his rage rather than relieve it. This balancing act of addressing and recognizing clients' overwhelming feelings while not unintentionally fueling them is part of the "art" of our work.

DEVELOPING YOUR ROADMAP: WHO ATTENDS EACH MEETING?

Some teams come together haphazardly at the start of a case. Clients retain attorneys and decide on a Collaborative model, the four people meet for the signing of the Participation Agreement, and the group sets off without thinking early on about their itinerary for the process and assuming they can call on allied team members as needed. We actually don't find this the most effective way to begin.

As we noted above, we encourage teams to hold a team call prior to the first meeting, and even if the only professionals on that call are two attorneys, we would encourage the team to think through who may be needed for this particular case, when might be the best time to introduce the clients to the idea of using additional professionals, and when might be the best time to bring in the actual professional—a coach (or coaches), a financial neutral, or a child specialist. During that first team call, team members can share their own philosophical approaches to team composition and functioning, so that differences in perspective can be discussed up front.

Unless you are two Collaborative attorneys completing a case without additional professionals, your team will inevitably make decisions along the way about which professionals to include in which meetings. As you move through the phases of the work, these decisions are sometimes complex. We suggest that they should be made by the whole team, with consideration of a number of factors.

Our guiding principle in deciding who should attend each meeting is the shared aim of maintaining as secure and effective a Macrocontainer as possible for both clients. As we've discussed previously, the Macrocontainer of the whole team allows both clients to feel safe, heard, cared for, and understood. When deciding if a meeting should include coaches or the financial neutral, the team first needs to consider whether the Macrocontainer will remain sturdy and effective if some of the Microcontainers are absent. For example, let's say in one case the husband is proceeding through the divorce with relative ease. He is confident about the future and feels ready to evaluate the options about spousal support and the sale of the house without the coaches present. If his wife is frightened of her financial future and grieving the upcoming sale of the house, the team may decide the coaches *must* be present, because without the crucial Microcontainer of *wife-and-coach*, the wife is likely to feel vulnerable, distressed, and unable to cognitively process options at the meeting.

As another example, consider a situation in which both clients want to work on brainstorming and option development without the financial neutral present in order to save money on his fees. Say these clients have a history of spending beyond their means and accumulating debt. Say their debt is about to skyrocket as they separate into two households. The attorneys may feel that the Macrocontainer of *attorneys—and a financial neutral* will be more effective in delivering bad news and helping the clients consider ways to cut expenses than the attorneys would be on their own. This situation could lead to a team decision to include the financial neutral, despite the fact that both clients prefer to exclude him.

Bottom line: decisions about who should be on a team and which team members should attend each meeting should grow out of a team discussion of the various factors, emotional and financial, that will maintain the container and help the clients complete the case successfully. All these decisions will need to be vetted with the clients and explained fully. If the team feels certain of the wisdom of their road map, they should present these suggestions with confidence and firmness. If the team feels there are pros and cons of their chosen way forward, that complexity should be reviewed with the clients as well.

Occasionally, a team may comply with a couple's strong preference to hold a meeting without certain team members present when the content of the meeting appears to be straightforward and emotionally tame. We have learned from making this very decision in a variety of cases that we cannot always predict accurately how a meeting will play out. Sometimes a team—and the clients—learn that the absence of a particular team member can have a surprisingly strong impact on the functioning of a group. In one case we know of a team was scheduled to hold a meeting in which they planned to review clients' budgets and expenses. As a cost-saving measure, and at the request of the clients, the team agreed to hold the meeting with only attorneys and the financial neutral present—not their sole neutral coach. By the end of the meeting, all five people present agreed the meeting had crawled along slowly and inefficiently. They missed the coach's expertise in structuring the time, keeping the professionals focused, and helping the clients articulate their concerns in a timely fashion. Time needed to be spent in the following meeting to complete the work, and everyone agreed to include the coach in all further meetings—even though the clients were proceeding amicably and were at ease.

An attorney colleague related to us a vignette in which she advocated strongly, over the protestation of the other attorney and both clients, to have the team's coach present at a financial meeting. When the coach was largely silent during the meeting, our colleague became anxious. Would the clients and the other attorney feel resentful at having agreed to include the coach? Had the coach brought any "value-added" to the meeting? Our colleague needn't have worried. After the meeting her client told her "I'm so glad our coach was here. Just having her there made me feel supported, safer, and more able to consider options." When in doubt about whether or not to include a team member in a particular meeting, we advocate erring on the side of inclusion.

▼▼▼▼▼

Deciding Which Professionals Should Attend Upcoming Meetings: Factors to Consider

- *Emotional dynamic of the clients*—the more volatile or unpredictable, the more essential it will be to include coaches in all meetings.
- *Emotional vulnerability or fragility of either client*—if either client is struggling with anxiety, grief, a sense of betrayal, depression, or a lack of confidence when facing his or her spouse, having a coach attend all meetings will be helpful.
- *Risk of emotional or organizational fallout versus benefit in cost saving* if a particular team member does not attend a given meeting.
- *Are there alternative options for cost saving* that might create less risk to client progress?
- *Input from each and every team member as well as both clients about how best to proceed.*

COLLABORATIVE TEAMS: FUNCTION AND DYSFUNCTION

6

HEALTHY TEAM FUNCTIONING

If you have been participating in Collaborative cases for some time, you probably know what it is like to be on a "great team" and what it is like to be on a "not-so-great team." Remember the famous Tolstoy line about all happy families being alike, while "each unhappy family is unhappy in its own way"? That principle holds true for Collaborative teams; good teams have a lot in common, but there are myriad ways a team can devolve. It's no wonder that Collaborative professionals who have the luxury of working repeatedly with colleagues they like and trust tend to do so. When we join a team with one or more unfamiliar members, we often feel anxious—we are in uncharted territory.

▼▼▼▼▼
Traits of Functional Teams

- There is open, honest, and trusting communication between professionals.

- There are regularly scheduled and frequent team calls or meetings.
- There is cohesion and respect among all the professionals.
- All team members have respect and compassion for *both* clients.
- There is a lack of hierarchy; all team members feel equally valued, regardless of discipline or level of experience.
- Each team member trusts all other members' competence and judgment.
- Team members are collegial; they *like* one another.
- Each team member is able to reflect on him- or herself and on the dynamics of the team, and to receive and give feedback in helpful ways.
- Team members share a desire to learn and evolve in their capacity to better serve their clients.
- Team members equally share a sense of responsibility for maintaining communication and completing tasks.

TEAM PROBLEMS ARE NORMAL

Earlier we explained that from time to time we all have negative countertransference reactions toward clients and our teammates. We made the point that these experiences are not only *going* to happen, they *need* to happen. It is only by getting pulled into intense emotional experiences and thinking our way out that we can come to understand our clients and learn how to be helpful to them. All working groups, including Collaborative teams, inevitably experience moments of tension between and among the various working relationships. People become discouraged, people disagree, people hold strong opinions and sometimes feel frustrated if teammates do not share

"It is the ability of the team to process these moments of tension and reach a shared understanding that sets a well-functioning team apart from those that struggle and flounder."

those opinions or are unable to listen well in a particular interaction. It is the ability of the team to process these moments of tension and reach a shared understanding that sets a well-functioning team apart from those that struggle and flounder. Just as clients can be understood as functioning along the Rigidity/Flexibility Continuum, so can all of us.

A good measure of a team's capacity to function well is how vigilant team members are in staying attuned to the undercurrents of client and interprofessional dynamics. When a team *is* tuned in, when it is actively reading the terrain of the river of a case as it flows downstream, problems tend to be transitory. The well-functioning team anticipates difficulty, and is quickly able to mobilize aspects of the Macrocontainer and the Microcontainer to process their difficulty and emerge more cohesive, with an enhanced understanding of their own (and the couple's) dynamics.

On the other hand, when teams are not tuned in, when they are unable to read the Collaborative river but rather are borne along by it in a state of stressful reactivity, team difficulties are repeated, compounded, and (eventually) entrenched. The primary focus of this chapter is the very nature of dysfunctional teams. Our hope is that by developing a greater understanding of what happens when teams get stuck, we can enhance our capacities to manage future team difficulties such that team functioning can be sustained and enhanced.

▼▼▼▼▼

An Example of an Important Question About Team Composition

The Sole Neutral Coach Model versus The Two Coach Model

The authors have been up front about our bias for a full-team approach including two mental health professionals. But, as we stated in the Introduction, we know that our current way of thinking about team composition is only one way, and we are always interested in ways that other successful

Collaborative practitioners are working. For example, we know from conversations with our colleagues in Texas, and our own working experience in Virginia, that many communities favor the "one-coach model" of practice. On a pragmatic level, of course, using a single mental health professional might save a family money in fees, pare down the complexity of team communications, render coordination of scheduling somewhat easier, and allow teams to form in areas where there are very few Collaboratively trained mental health professionals.

In evaluating the efficacy of the use of one mental health professional versus two mental health professionals, we must consider the direct impact of our decision on the very nature of the role of the mental health professional(s) at the table. The fact that different geographic areas use different titles for this role is our first indication that when we talk about a "sole coach," a "neutral coach," a "neutral facilitator," or a "process facilitator," we actually may be describing significantly different team roles and functions. For example, the title "neutral coach" suggests a person who will maintain an unbiased position while working with both clients in an encouraging, supportive manner. The term "process facilitator" suggests that the mental health professional will remain primarily focused on communication between professionals and on moving the process along efficiently. We believe that the more thoughtful a community and an individual team are about how they define the role of their own mental health professional(s) (in fact, about the role of each member of their team), the more effectively they will function.

Our own experience is that clients who fall on the more rigid end of the Rigidity/Flexibility Continuum generally benefit from having their own dedicated coach. We find that these clients often have difficulty holding on to the idea that a professional is in fact neutral, particularly when that professional says something that challenges—intentionally or unintentionally—the client's point of view. Once a neutral facilitator—or a sole coach—is seen as biased or unempathic, that professional faces an uphill battle in his or her attempts to hold on to a working alliance with both members of the couple.

On the other hand, we have learned through conversations with highly skilled Collaborative professionals who work as sole coaches or neutral facilitators that, on some teams, their neutrality makes it less likely that they will be experienced by clients and/or team members as allied with one client over the other. They describe that a mental health professional's neutrality can, in some cases, have a positive impact not only on adversarial clients, but on adversarial professionals.

While it is our experience that the strongest Collaborative container includes a dedicated coach for each party, we are intrigued by the idea that for some clients and teams a sole neutral mental health professional might be the better choice. We look forward to participating in this ongoing debate about how best to form the highest-functioning teams.

TEAM DYSFUNCTION: THE INTERACTION OF CLIENT DYNAMICS AND TEAM DYNAMICS

We can organize the nature of team difficulties into two general categories. In the first category are problems that originate in a vulnerability of one or more of the professionals, such as low skill level, poor recollection, misunderstanding of the law, rigidity of character, and professional-owned countertransferences (such as substantial failures of empathy, or dislike or idealization of one member of the couple). In the second category are

▼

"We can organize the nature of team difficulties into two general categories . . . problems that originate in a vulnerability of one or more of the professionals . . . and problems that flow from client-induced countertransferences . . . ."

team problems that flow from client-induced countertransferences (such as ordinary levels of irritation, or a passing overidentification with one client).

Certain couples make it hard for even an experienced and cohesive team to remain centered. High-conflict marital patterns can be toxic. They can work their way into us and into our team dynamics, threatening both our personal equilibrium and the integrity of our Micro- and Macrocontainers. Faced with clients who frequently become strenuously positional, who consistently express powerfully negative emotion, or who stubbornly under- or overreact leaves us vulnerable to behaving in those ways ourselves. When we become fatigued, anxious, confused, or angry with our clients or with one another, we lose our capacity to speak calmly and directly, maintain open and equal communication, think nonjudgmentally, and remain creative and thoughtful.

Why do teams sometimes start to look like their clients? Let's think back to our discussion of projection. In Chapter 2 we explored the way in which couples seek to establish homeostasis by projecting uncomfortable aspects of themselves into each other. We described how, when couples separate, they become emotionally destabilized. In an attempt to regain psychic homeostasis, each member of the couple seeks new recipients for their projections in other important people in their lives—including their Collaborative professionals.

When a powerful projection from a client "finds a home" in one or more team members (that is, when the projection is aimed at a team member, and the team member takes it in and finds him- or herself behaving in extreme or uncharacteristic ways), some aspect of the marital dynamic will become reenacted within the team. When this happens, there is frequently a ripple effect; as one or more members of the Collaborative team get pulled out of orbit, others will often follow. Consider this example:

Mandy grew up abused by her parents. She saw herself as unlovable and worthless. In her marriage, she projected this vision of herself as unlovable onto her spouse, and repeatedly—but often unfairly—accused him of mistreating her. She often behaved in provocative ways that elicited his frustration and annoyance, which confirmed to Mandy that her husband did not love her. When she and her husband separated and Mandy began working closely with a Collaborative attorney and coach, she soon began to project this same vision of herself onto them, accusing them of mistreating and disliking her. She began behaving in angry and unreasonable ways when interacting with these professionals, thereby eliciting their impatience and frustration. Because of their irritation with her, Mandy's professionals began to avoid checking in with her between meetings and were slow to respond to her calls and e-mails. This made Mandy even angrier. She acted out badly in team meetings. Mandy's husband, as well as his coach and attorney, began to feel that Mandy's professionals were being avoidant and ineffectual.

> "When a powerful projection from a client 'finds a home' in one or more team members . . . some aspect of the marital dynamic will become reenacted within the team."

Soon the team had two "sides," one feeling angry and frustrated, one attacked and defensive. Voila: Mandy's individual emotional difficulty (feeling unlovable and worthless), which had been stabilized in her marital dynamic (projecting her own sense of herself into her husband such that she experienced him as abusive) had worked its way into the team. Now it was Mandy's coach and attorney who had provoked anger in the husband's coach and attorney, and it was Mandy's coach and attorney who felt unappreciated and worthless.

We now are going to describe a number of common team dysfunction patterns, all of which are manifestations of the phenomenon of projection by the client(s) inducing countertransference reactions in the professional(s). In most cases, the difficulties that arise out of these patterns are transitory in nature. Often the professional(s) involved will notice the problem and either think it through alone or talk it through with a colleague and correct course. Sometimes, when a team finds itself repeatedly caught up in unproductive interactions, they will schedule a phone conference or face-to-face meeting with the purpose of developing a shared understanding of what's happening. When these conversations go well, they become powerful opportunities for enhanced understanding and growth.

Despite a team's best efforts, difficulties in relationships between team members and/or between clients and team members can become entrenched and immutable. When this unfortunate scenario unfolds, it is usually because one or more members of the professional team has a personality at the rigid end of the Rigidity/Flexibility Continuum and is unable to reflect on his or her own feelings and behavior or give credence to the differing perceptions of others.

▼▼▼▼▼

Ingredients That Contribute to Team Dysfunction

In Professionals

Rigidity
Incompetence
Unavailability/unresponsiveness to the team
Lack of self-reflection, insight
Adversarial approach
Negative transference towards a team member
Negative countertransference towards a client
Splitting

In Clients

High conflict dynamic
Negative transference to team member or whole team
Rigidity
Symptoms of mental disorder
Lack of self-reflection, insight
Splitting

COMMON PATTERNS OF TEAM DYSFUNCTION

THE DIVIDED TEAM

You have probably noticed that groups, when faced with tough interpersonal challenges, often splinter. It's natural: when one or more members of the group feel attacked, blamed, or insecure, they often attempt to isolate another team member and enlist her as an ally who can join with them, validate them, and help them to feel less alienated. This happens in families, social groups, and professional working groups—including Collaborative teams. Mental health professionals call this drawing in of a third person to strengthen one side of a conflict or debate "triangulation." A struggle between two people (or one person and a group of others) thus becomes an interaction between three contingents.

EXAMPLE OF TRIANGULATION LEADING TO TEAM DIVISION

(To help our readers avoid confusion about this cast of characters, we will have an "E Team," which includes Eliza (the wife), Elaine (her attorney), and Ellie (her coach) and a "J Team," which includes John (the husband), Josephine (his attorney), and Jeff (his coach).

Elaine gets a call from her client, Eliza. Eliza wants more money this month than the interim support payment that her husband, John, has provided. Eliza feels entitled to an extra $1,000 and is angry when Elaine explains that a change in the interim support amount would need to be discussed at the next team meeting. Eliza "loses it" on the phone to Elaine, and shifts from anxious tearfulness to accusatory anger at Elaine's failure to advocate sufficiently for her needs.

After the call ends, Elaine e-mails Josephine and explains that Eliza is upset, scared about her inability to pay her bills, and anxious to the point that she cannot make it to the next team meeting without additional funds from John. Josephine e-mails back, annoyed. She responds that Eliza's overspending is an ongoing bad habit and that, obviously, there is no appropriate way to address this until the issue can be raised at the next meeting. Josephine says, "it doesn't feel fair to me to ask John to change an interim agreement between meetings just because Eliza is throwing a tantrum—again."

After reading Josephine's e-mail, Elaine is both irritated at Josephine and anxious about being the object of Eliza's anger and dissatisfaction. She calls Eliza's coach, Ellie. The two women discuss the situation, Elaine relating that she had found Josephine's e-mail to have a "snarky" tone, and that she believed Josephine should have behaved more "collaboratively" by helping Elaine think of some way to manage the financial tensions between John and Eliza—or perhaps by offering to talk to John about Eliza's anxiety about paying her bills. Elaine notes to Ellie that Josephine seems overly judgmental of Eliza, and that Eliza's awareness of Josephine's judgmentalness is damaging to the case.

Ellie listens sympathetically to Elaine and agrees that Josephine seems critical of Eliza, and that it would be more helpful to the team's work together if Josephine could understand how frightened Eliza is of being financially strapped. It would be more helpful still if Josephine could work harder to help John feel more generous and empathic toward Eliza. Ellie adds that she has worked with Josephine on cases before, and that Josephine tends to be irritable when the situation calls for scheduling additional meetings or having team discussions between meetings. Ellie shares that she experiences this quality of Josephine's character as "a pain in the neck." Ellie offers to call Jeff, John's coach, to see if Jeff has any ideas for how to talk to John about giving Eliza some extra money this month before the next meeting.

Elaine gets off the phone with Ellie feeling vindicated in her annoyance with Josephine, reassured that she is not alone in coping with Eliza's anger, and supported in her wish to get John to give Eliza some extra money this month (so that Eliza will back off of her attack on Elaine). Josephine has no idea that Ellie plans to speak with Jeff about this issue—until she receives an e-mail from Jeff explaining that he has received a call from Ellie. He complains to Josephine about Ellie's lack of understanding about John, and about Elaine's wish to pressure John in order to appease Eliza. Jeff and Josephine share a bonding moment while they complain about Elaine and Ellie. Meanwhile, Ellie and Elaine feel closer to one another and strengthened in their resolve to support Eliza's interests.

Remind you of junior high? Yes, this team has now been—for the moment, at any rate—divided. Eliza's team—Elaine and Ellie— are shoring each other up in their views and their preferences for how to handle the clients' dynamic, while John's team, Josephine and Jeff, have unified around their own set of complaints about Elaine and Ellie. The team as a whole has turned into a two-on-two skirmish, with each team focusing on its complaints about the other professionals instead of on how to help the clients with their current challenges. Rather than seeking ballast and balance from the team as a whole, Elaine sought her own equilibrium by triangulating with Ellie—and Ellie fell for it.

No one on the team has taken a step back yet, to notice that Eliza's anxiety and entitlement are being projected into her attorney. Nor have they noticed that the team needs to come together to talk about how to handle John and Eliza's dynamics around money and patterns of coping with anxiety. If Elaine had asked her team for a team conference call after Eliza's tearful, accusatory call to her, the team could have put their heads together to observe that their clients' old marital dynamics around budgeting and spending were being triggered by their current interim support agreement. Ellie and Jeff might have talked about John's worry about Eliza's overspending and Eliza's deep-seated fears about being poor and unable to pay her bills. Josephine and Elaine could have conferred about how Elaine might respond to Eliza's latest demand, and the team as a whole might have come up with some options for how to help the couple move forward to the next meeting, without having any one professional bear the brunt of Eliza's anger. If the team had come together to face the couple's dynamics, Elaine would have felt supported, Ellie and Jeff would have worked together to help both attorneys understand and empathize with both clients, and Josephine and Elaine would have felt better able to work collaboratively to both represent their own client's needs while simultaneously and compassionately attending to the other client's fears.

If the pattern of divided communication described in the above scenario repeats over time throughout the process of John and Eliza's divorce, their Collaborative team will become increasingly rancorous and mistrusting of one another. They will have increasing difficulty working together to create a sense of safety and cohesion in their work with their clients. Completing this case—if in fact they can manage that—will not be enjoyable or rewarding. Instead of the four professionals emerging from this experience appreciating one another and admiring each other's skills, they will move back into their communities with ill will and a "bad taste in their mouths"—possibly about the Collaborative process, and certainly about each other.

Meanwhile, the marital problems about budgeting and spending, about entitlement and angry withholding, and about mutual mistrust will go unaddressed and unchanged as Eliza and John get divorced and move into their futures. Eliza will never have the opportunity to look at how to plan her monthly budget in more effective ways, nor at how to understand the panic that sets in when she sees her bank balance dwindling—even when there is actually enough money in it to meet her expenses. John will never be asked to look at his part in the dynamic—his original choice to marry a woman who was dependent and needy so he could feel powerful and in control, and his growing resentment at having to carry the responsibility of being the sole breadwinner—which he had historically expressed by withholding both money and affection from his wife. Even if they are able to reach agreement within the Collaborative process, they are likely to look back on the model as significantly flawed, and the experience as unpleasant. If a divided team cannot find a way to identify their dysfunctional pattern and correct course to regain their cohesion, their clients may ultimately come to see the Collaborative process with cynicism, feeling that the professionals "talked the talk" but didn't "walk the walk."

> "If a divided team cannot find a way to identify their dysfunctional pattern and correct course to regain their cohesion, their clients may ultimately come to see the Collaborative process with cynicism, feeling that the professionals 'talked the talk' but didn't 'walk the walk.'"

THE ROGUE PROFESSIONAL

The rogue professional is a team member who gradually develops an emotional overidentification with a client that drives that professional toward positional behavior and slowly creates a wall between that professional and the rest of his or her teammates. A few factors are generally present when a Collaborative professional "goes rogue." One, the professional finds it easy to relate to the client and likes him or her personally. Two, the professional identifies in some way with the client's interests, and quickly begins to see things from the client's perspective. Three, the professional finds it easy to feel antipathy toward the client's spouse and is unsympathetic to his or her point of view. And four, the professional is inherently

> "Professionals who 'go rogue' develop reactions to a client and feelings about their client's interests that are rooted in their own earlier history and relationships—and they have trouble recognizing that their countertransference has been activated."

vulnerable to feeling either excluded or picked-on by others with whom he or she works. If you are thinking back to our discussion of countertransference, you are right on the money. Professionals who go rogue develop reactions to a client and feelings about their client's interests that are rooted in their own earlier history and relationships—and they have trouble recognizing that their countertransference has been activated.

EXAMPLE OF A TEAM PROFESSIONAL'S COUNTERTRANSFERENCE LEADING TO HIS GOING ROGUE

Mark, an attorney, found that he felt protective of his client Barb from the moment he met her. Although she was at least ten years older than he, Barb seemed drawn to Mark like an orphan in a storm: lost, frightened, timid, and in need of guidance and a solid protector. Although Mark was a dedicated Collaborative attorney and had worked on a number of successful teams, he found, during the first few team conference calls on this case, that he felt annoyed with the attorney and coach who were working with Larry, Barb's husband. Mark felt that the other professions didn't grasp the way in which Larry bullied Barb. He felt that Larry's attorney was judgmental about Barb's spending habits. On one call Mark was surprised when Larry's coach, Karen, noted that Mark sounded defensive. Mark felt Karen was patronizing him. When Mark spoke to Barb after the team call, he noted to her that Larry had a "tough team" and that he was determined to make sure her needs were protected going forward so she did not have to feel so anxious about her financial future. He even went so far as to tell her that at some point he would sit down with her to strategize how much spousal support to ask for so she could be sure of getting a liberal amount. Barb felt grateful to Mark, and commented that it felt reassuring to have a "white knight" at her side.

Meanwhile, Larry's attorney and coach mentioned to Barb's coach (when they ran into her at a meeting for another case) that they felt Mark was sounding "awfully positional" and that he seemed to view Larry in a negative light. They worried that Mark viewed his client, Barb, as the victim. Barb's coach offered to check in with Mark, and to try to help him regain a more balanced view of both clients. But when Barb's coach reached out to Mark, Mark again felt attacked. He surmised that she had been talking behind his back with Larry's team. The conversation with Barb's coach left Mark feeling more isolated from the rest of the team, and more determined than ever to be Barb's one loyal representative at the table. He decided that since Barb's coach seemed more aligned with Larry than with her own client, Mark would make himself more available to Barb for emotional support (essentially acting as both attorney and coach). As Mark began to create a stronger, but also more separate, bond with Barb in the case, Barb stopped returning her own coach's phone calls. In turn, Barb's coach began to feel pushed aside and to view Mark's behavior as harmful to the process. She hypothesized that Mark was caught up in his own countertransference feelings toward Barb. However, when she tried to gently raise this idea during a team debrief after a meeting, Mark became annoyed. He expressed a sense that the whole team was bent on obstructing the legal rights of his client and acquiescing to the needs of Larry.

If Mark had possessed the capacity to reflect on his own reactions and feelings toward Barb and the other team members, he might have been able to recognize the ways in which his behavior in this case reflected his earlier experience in relationships. Mark's own father had died when Mark was 9, and the boy had been very close to his mother, whom he worried about throughout his adolescence. She remarried when Mark was 15, and Mark experienced his stepfather as an unwelcome intruder. When his mother and stepfather divorced seven years later, Mark's mother leaned heavily on her son for emotional support. Mark enjoyed his role as his mother's confidant. Now, in this Collaborative case, Mark was unable to recognize the ways in which Barb triggered in him a response very like the one he had had with his own mother. Because it felt familiar to him, he fell easily into the role of Barb's confidant and champion. Mark also failed to realize that Larry triggered in him the old feelings of anger and mistrust that he had felt toward his stepfather.

In the case described above, Mark found himself wandering into emotional territory that was evocative of powerful relationship patterns and feelings that he had internalized as a child and adolescent. He then saw the dynamics of his case through the distorting filter of his own early experience. Whenever a professional begins to see a client or couple in black-and-white terms (rather than shades of gray), the rest of the team inevitably (and appropriately) responds with concern. When the team expresses their concern and finds that their colleague is unable or unwilling to explore the roots of the difficulty, the team inevitably becomes frustrated and worried.

In addition to wreaking havoc in the team, the rogue professional's behaviors and the team's reactions to them can contribute—and actually intensify—old patterns in the couple that led to their divorce. Using the example of Mark, Barb, and Larry, we can imagine that Mark's protective stance might well increase Barb's historic belief that when Larry is critical of her behavior, he is being "a bully." She might then feel absolved of the need to explore her own motivations or choices. Mark's way of relating to Barb and to his team members might, in turn, make Larry uneasy and suspicious, thus eliciting less flexible behavior from him. In this way, the negative interactional patterns of the couple would intensify as the Collaborative process continued, with an attendant deterioration of their ability to collaborate. A successful resolution would become increasingly unlikely.

Striking a good balance between working autonomously with our clients and coordinating our work with the rest of the team is sometimes a challenge. With particularly anxious or needy clients, we often find ourselves spending hours per week on the phone or in meetings helping them to manage their emotions. This can feel like a full-time job, and we don't necessarily think (or have energy) to fill in our teammates on a regular basis. By contrast, we might develop particularly warm relationships with clients to whom we relate extremely well. Our conversations with these folks—the ones we connect with immediately, come to like tremendously, and toward whom we feel particularly "simpatico"—might also begin to develop a life outside of team interaction. Whether because of the draining nature of our relationship to a given client or because the relationship is particularly gratifying, we want to keep an eye on ways that our ongoing conversations with and understanding of our client might evolve into a parallel, rather than intersecting, path with other team discussion. In that way we can avoid being (or appearing to be) overidentified or aligned with our client. If we do fall out of alignment with our team, and we become aware of that ourselves or a team member points it out, we can avoid falling into a rogue dynamic.

By now we've made the point several times: all of us will, at various points in our work, get pulled into our client's dynamics in potentially difficult ways. If we are able to reflect, say, on a way in which we have become overidentified with a client, if we can rely on our team to help us regain our objectivity, we will be fine. A well-functioning team will be responsive to our requests for help, will share our curiosity about the relationship between the clients' and the team's dynamics, and will offer helpful feedback about our own perceptions and behavior. In this way, what might have become a countertransference "problem" can be transformed into an opportunity for growth for us, for the team, and for the clients. What distinguishes a rogue professional from any one of us is that when he or she is drawn into countertransference reactions to clients, those reactions can never be brought into the professional's awareness. Like the rigid client, the rogue professional experiences feedback from the team as a critical attack that simply pushes him or her further into a rigid, polarized position.

> "A well-functioning team will be responsive to our requests for help, will share our curiosity about the relationship between the clients' and the team's dynamics, and will offer helpful feedback about our own perceptions and behavior. In this way, what might have been a countertransference 'problem' can be transformed into an opportunity for growth . . ."

THE VILIFIED CLIENT

We have now talked about two forms of team dynamics that lead to discord in the team, challenge team cohesion, and can contribute to the couple's ongoing dysfunction. A third pattern that we often see in teams is one in which the entire team coalesces around one client and develops antipathy toward the other. This pattern frequently develops early on in the case. It often begins with seemingly benign joking between team members—lighthearted commentary about which of us "drew the short straw," "is going to have an uphill battle," or "got lucky this time."

When the team begins to see one client as the less healthy member of the couple, there is usually a basis in reality. One client may be more limited in self-awareness, less able to compromise, more emotionally reactive, and more difficult to talk with— that is, closer to the rigid end of the Continuum. If a team is not careful to avoid developing a stronger alliance with the healthier (more flexible) client along with an attendant disdain for the more rigid client, the team can find itself functioning like a social club that has blackballed an applicant.

> "If a team is not careful to avoid developing a stronger alliance with the healthier (more flexible) client along with an attendant disdain for the more rigid client, the team can find itself functioning like a social club that has blackballed an applicant."

Consider this example:

Before the first team meeting with George and Carlos, a couple who had been partnered for eight years, George's attorney and coach warned the rest of the team that George would be the challenging figure in the case. "Whatever you do," commented George's coach, "do not smile or crack any kind of joke during this meeting, or George will have a melt down. He is coming into this meeting loaded for bear." "No kidding," added his attorney. "If you see his face getting red . . . duck!" Everybody laughed.

As the meeting got under way, George did become irritated a number of times. At one point he snapped, "No, thank you," when Carlos's attorney offered him a plate of cookies, adding, "This isn't

*some kind of party. This is the worst day of my life and I don't even
want to be here, let alone eating cookies." George talked at length
throughout the meeting, while Carlos said little. George punctuated his
discussion of his goals and interests with barbed comments, such as
"I want to stay in the house. Somebody needs to take care of our son
and it's obviously going to have to be me." Carlos, by contrast, noted
that he wanted "the best for George" and that he hoped the two would
be able to maintain a friendship after their divorce. George reacted to
this sentiment with a derisive snort and a muttered "Fat chance."*

*By the time the meeting and the team debrief were over, the
professionals were exhausted. They felt they had had to walk on
eggshells throughout the meeting in order to contain George and not
provoke or exacerbate his outbursts. George's coach noted that he
felt nothing but sympathy for Carlos, a seemingly quiet and unassum-
ing man, and Carlos's attorney noted that George was going to need
reining-in by his team in order to keep him from dominating meetings
with his selfish needs.*

*No one on the team thought to wonder what had drawn these
clients together in the first place. The team failed to note Carlos's passivity, and the fact that George's aggression tended to escalate when
Carlos failed to respond even to reasonable questions or comments.
Although they had accused George of being "loaded for bear," it was
actually the team that had brought preconceptions to the work. They
were well on their way to vilifying George, slipping into a pattern
of seeing him as the "bad guy" without consideration of the marital
dynamic (the Lock and Key between the two members of the couple).
Over time, as George sensed more of the team's impatience and disdain, George became more extreme and rigid. In turn, Carlos became
increasingly less sympathetic and less generous toward George. Thus,
the team's dynamic reinforced the couple's, and the goal of reaching
agreement receded further from reach.*

How does a team avoid getting stuck feeling positively toward
one client and negatively toward the other when one client is actually more overtly likeable than the other? How does each professional avoid skewing his or her collaborative alliance toward the
client who is more reasonable and cooperative, and away from the
client who is more stubborn and vengeful?

We can avoid vilifying one client (and idealizing the other) by reminding ourselves that clients choose each other for important reasons. Often, they collude in a dynamic in which one of them *looks* sicker or more difficult, but they each contribute toward the difficulty between them. By remaining tuned in to (and attempting to understand) the equally important role that each member plays in his or her part in the duet, we can more easily generate empathy for the less likeable client. And remember: this is a particularly hard time for both clients. Under conditions of stress people's characterological vulnerabilities (and their couple dynamics) become exaggerated.

> "We can avoid vilifying one client (and idealizing the other) by reminding ourselves that clients choose each other for important reasons. Often, they collude in a dynamic in which one of them looks sicker or more difficult, but they each contribute toward the difficulty between them."

We've made the point several times that the key to healthy team functioning is openness. If any team member notices the team favoring one client over the other, that professional will serve the whole team—and both clients—by pointing it out. Never shy away from reminding yourself and your team that every couple has its own shared dynamic; both members of the couple contribute equally (if not equally obviously) to their difficulties. Share your knowledge of your clients' lives with your team members; keeping our clients' histories in mind helps us to work together to understand our clients' behaviors. And here's a secret: once you know someone very well, it's hard not to like him (or at least feel empathy for him).

> "Share your knowledge of your client's lives with your team members; keeping our clients' histories in mind helps us to work together to understand our clients' behaviors. And here's a secret: once you know someone very well, it's hard not to like him (or at least feel empathy for him)."

Finally, remember: this is work, it is not personal. At the end of the day, you can close your case file, hang up the phone, turn off your computer. When a client provokes your anger, impatience,

▼

"As hard as it is to interact with your difficult client, it is much harder to *be* them. Imagine living in a persecutory world of your own creation—repeatedly alienating even those who are predisposed to want to help you."

or disdain, remind yourself— they do this *all the time*, not just to you. As hard as it is to interact with your difficult client, it is much harder to *be* them. Imagine living in a persecutory aworld of your own creation—repeatedly alienating even those who are predisposed to want to help you.

TEAM DYNAMICS: A SUMMARY

If you have been practicing as a Collaborative professional, we have no doubt that you have experienced other types of team dynamics that are problematic and obstruct the team as a whole from helping the clients most effectively. Some teams (particularly less experienced ones) underfunction or are driven to behave in unproductive ways by intimidatingly formidable clients. Other teams overfunction, eclipsing less self-directed clients by monopolizing meetings, or taking over the process of option generation and evaluation. Some teams suffer from poor communication all around, and some teams struggle with one team member who brings little to the table or is distant and unavailable. Whatever dysfunctional pattern you encounter, we encourage you to make whatever efforts you can to *name* it—either in vivo, or later after some thought and consideration. We encourage you to read Sharon Ellison's book *Taking the War Out of Words*, which is packed with helpful guidance about how to start and conduct difficult conversations. Whether you are trying to raise awareness about skewed alliances, enhance poor communication, rein in rogue behavior, or ease divisive tension, effective communication is the key.

We have all been in the hot seat. Hearing supportive criticism or receiving guidance from a more experienced professional about how to be more effective can be emotionally challenging. Still, if we can keep our egos in check, these are important learning moments. If you have found yourself at odds with teammates on numerous occasions, or if you have repeatedly received negative feedback from other professionals, we encourage you to take a look at yourself. Ask yourself: are you carrying unhelpful personal baggage into your work? Try to be curious about your own emotional triggers. If you come to believe that team problems often originate with you, get support. Consult

▼

"Ask yourself: are you carrying unhelpful personal baggage into your work? Try to be curious about your own emotional triggers."

a trusted colleague or seek counseling. Ours is emotionally fraught and challenging work—we all need help to do it well.

FUNCTIONAL TEAM

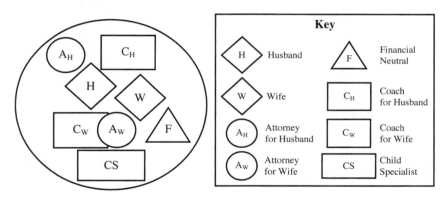

Fundamental characteristics include:

1. The team is aware of the couple's dynamic and its impact on the team.
2. The team is cohesive.
3. All team members feel equal to one another.
4. Team members communicate regularly with one another and uphold the full and open disclosure clause of the Participation Agreement.
5. Team members work in a coordinated fashion for the best interests of both clients and the whole family.

6. Team members remain aware of their own reactions to the clients and work together to maintain a safe container for both clients.
7. Successful outcomes for the clients are likely.

DIVIDED TEAM

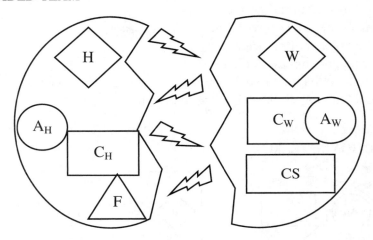

Fundamental characteristics include:

1. Team professionals do not remain aware of clients' dynamics of splitting and adversarial positioning but instead begin to mirror that dynamic.
2. The team begins to divide into two adversarial subgroups with each client's own "side" feeling strongly allied with that client and suspicious or less supportive of the other client and his or her team professionals.
3. The team loses cohesion and members lose trust in one another.
4. Communication between wife's "side" and husband's "side" becomes strained and deteriorates.
5. Neutrals on the team begin to feel pulled into an alliance with one client over the other.
6. Successful outcomes for the clients become less likely.

VILIFIED CLIENT

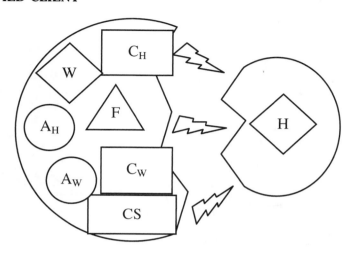

Fundamental characteristics include:

1. Team professionals do not remain aware of clients' dynamics in which one spouse takes on "victim" role in relationship and other spouse takes on "perpetrator/abuser" role, but instead begin to mirror that dynamic in their own perceptions of the couple.
2. The team begins to view one client as blameworthy and as less deserving of team empathy and support.
3. The team begins to favor the other client, often becoming overprotective of that client or overfunctioning on his or her behalf.
4. Successful outcomes for the clients become less likely.

ROGUE PROFESSIONAL

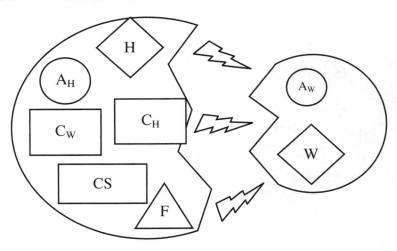

Fundamental characteristics include:

1. One team member loses his or her awareness of the couple's dynamics and of his or her own reactions to those dynamics.
2. That team member becomes overidentified with and protective of his or her own client and loses a balanced vision of the case and couple.
3. That team member begins to feel that the rest of the team and/or the other client is behaving in an unfair manner toward his or her own client and begins to take on adversarial positions on behalf of that client and against the rest of the team.
4. The rest of the team begins to lose trust in the rogue professional and the cohesion of the team deteriorates.
5. The rogue professional begins to communicate with his or her own client in ways that are not shared with the rest of the team, and full and open disclosure throughout the team is impaired or threatened.
6. Successful outcomes for the clients become less likely.

"LAND MINES" IN COLLABORATIVE PRACTICE 7

Challenges to the Collaborative process—highly charged situations that arise in a case, interrupt the flow of the meetings, and threaten to impede or implode our work—are common. They come in a wide variety of forms and present with a range of intensities. While ordinary challenges are often present (or predictable) from the beginning (think of a highly emotional and fragile client who reacts strongly and impulsively during meetings and requires continual deft management by the professionals), other challenges emerge suddenly and are acute and explosive. The latter often take us by surprise, seeming to come from out of the blue. In our Introduction, we invoked the river rafting metaphor as a way of conveying the general experience of Collaborative practice. In this chapter we are going to switch to a new metaphor, one we find helpful in describing the challenges of navigating when the Collaborative terrain feels particularly dangerous—the Collaborative "land mine."

Whether we see them on the horizon or stumble on them unknowingly, land mines feel big and scary; they pack an emotional wallop. Some land mines are relatively small and have only transitory fallout. Others are like nuclear bombs, causing great pain to our clients and great stress to the team. These are the land mines that put the most strain on both the Microcontainer and the Macrocontainer, and require each team member to use every tool in their Collaborative toolbox. Still, handled with skill and care, land mines can often be defused.

"Whether we see them on the horizon or stumble on them unknowingly, land mines feel big and scary; they pack an emotional wallop. Some land mines are relatively small and have only transitory fallout. Others are like nuclear bombs, causing great pain to our clients and great stress to the team."

Remember: We are not now describing the commonly tough aspects of our work, such as the ordinary moments during meetings when a client feels particularly angry, distressed, scared, or vengeful. While those moments pack their own punch and often require sensitive and skillful handling, we are focusing now on the enormously challenging situations that require special coordination and thoughtfulness.

As you read, keep in mind that the more cohesively a team can function in approaching a land mine, the greater the likelihood that the team will enable the clients to reach a safe and successful outcome within the process. To expand our metaphor a bit: when you spot the signs of a land mine ahead or when you are caught in the blast, slow down, stay alert, remain thoughtful, don't panic, and use your teammates. We will develop these ideas as we explore this more fully below.

"The more cohesively a team can function in approaching a land mine, the greater the likelihood that the team will enable the clients to reach a safe and successful outcome within the process."

Common Land Mines

- Reactions to disclosure of any emotionally provocative information previously hidden from the spouse (affairs, hidden debt or assets, substance abuse, paternity questions)
- Reactions to romantic relationships, past or present
- Reactions to one spouse's "coming out" with respect to sexual identity or sexual orientation
- Reactions to stressful changes in circumstance (such as job loss, financial reverses, financial windfalls)
- Reactions to diagnosis of serious illness in a client or a client's child
- Onset of clinical depression, acute anxiety, other mood disorder, or other mental illness; relapse of substance abuse disorder
- Incident of domestic violence or abuse, or accusations of such behavior
- Threats to terminate the Collaborative process, by one or both clients
- Threats to terminate one or more team members, by one or both clients

We can't address the specifics of dealing with *every* type of land mine. Even if space allowed, we couldn't do it—all clients and all teams are unique; we encounter new contingencies all the time. Fortunately, the authors believe that if we offer you a conceptual template for coping with explosive issues *in general,* you will easily be able to apply that template to the specific land mines that you encounter in your work.

CLASP: AN APPROACH TO MANAGING COLLABORATIVE LAND MINES

When our clients become emotionally overwhelmed and lose perspective, we tend to follow suit. At best we become frazzled, at worst we become overwhelmed and disorganized. Under this kind of strain, we often find ourselves sniping at teammates, interrupting each other with impatient tones, or becoming angry or overwrought in meetings—team cohesion begins to deteriorate at the very moment that it is most important. It is only by coming together as a unified team with the shared goal of guiding our clients to a safe destination that we can survive a sudden crisis in the Collaborative process. How do we maintain team integrity in the face of a land mine? Regardless of the nature of a land mine in a given case, there are steps to take that will increase your chances of successful navigation to the other side of the difficulty.

We have developed the following acronym to capture these steps:

CLASP

> **Coordinate** with team members.
> **Locate** the problem.
> **Anticipate** the potential benefits or fallout of various approaches to managing the land mine.
> **Support** one another as a team.
> **Plan** your next steps.

Now let's look at these steps one at a time.

Coordinating with our teammates when we detect trouble or sense that it's coming is crucial. Signs of trouble can come in any number of forms. Perhaps your client tells you that her spouse has relapsed after six months of sobriety. Maybe both clients are already working through the fact that your client has "come out" as gay, but now, a few months into their divorce process, your client discloses to you that he is seriously involved with a same-sex partner and intends to introduce that partner to the children soon. In such instances, the professional who first learns of the difficult (or potentially difficult) issue or situation should make clear to his or her client that a discussion with the rest of the team, and with the other client, will be essential. The "front line" professional should then speak to at least one of the other professionals right away, or call a team conference call to discuss the situation and consider next steps. Coordinating the flow of information in a thoughtful manner is the first task. If you are among the first to learn of the issue, you will want to think through the implications of sharing the information with only your "side" of the team first, or alternatively calling everyone together on a call to share it all at once (we will talk a bit more below about the sticky issues that arise when coordinating the communication flow of long-held secrets).

During the conversations with other team members, the remaining steps of the CLASP model should be discussed. **Locating** the problem includes defining and identifying the various aspects of the issue that are relevant to the divorce, examining the emotionally provocative implications of putting the issue on the table, and exploring the meaning, motivations, and underlying feelings that may be at work for either client. Once you feel you have a good understanding of the issue, the emotions driving the issue, and the interests or needs contained in the issue, you will be oriented and ready to think about how to proceed.

At this point you can turn to **anticipating** the implications of your client's situation or actions, and any impact the issue or information will have on the other client and the case. We often will want to imagine how circumstances may play out if we approach the difficulty from various angles, and consider more than one option for how to help our clients address the challenge. The anticipation work of CLASP is similar to generating and evaluating options. But here the team is doing the work, with a focus on how different paths might play out for our clients and for their process.

Supporting one another is always important and helpful, but when the team faces a difficult situation or a crisis, maintaining a patient, empathic stance vis-à-vis our teammates becomes critical. The more provocative the challenge in a case and the more difficult the clients are to manage (the more rigid their characters), the more important it is that we work to build a supportive emotional environment within the team itself. These are the times when our countertransference reactions are most likely to be triggered, and when we are most vulnerable to losing our objectivity and our ability to think carefully and slowly. If we are able to support one another rather than fall into positional or adversarial behavior ourselves, we will be able to move effectively into the final step in the CLASP sequence, which is planning—together—what next steps the team feels are most appropriate to help our clients proceed and, hopefully, remain in the Collaborative process.

Planning includes a determination of what homework may need to be done before the clients and team can fully understand, appropriately address, and work through the explosive material. If the issue is a financial one, documents or other forms of clarifying financial data might be needed. If the issue is related to an extramarital affair, a deeper exploration of the facts might be indicated. If the issue relates to the onset of a mental disorder or a relapse of addictive behavior, the team may want their client to be assessed by an outside mental health professional.

Planning will also include helping each client to prepare for a joint conversation that openly addresses the provocative issue; we will talk more about these preparatory sessions in a moment. The road map that the team carefully creates to help the clients navigate safely through an explosive moment in their process will vary in shape, sequence, and direction. What we hope our readers will remember when a tough challenge pops up is the general CLASP approach, which—in simple terms—advises that a team take time, take stock, and take care of one another as it helps the clients work through their difficulty.

LAND MINE EXAMPLE # 1: DISCLOSURE OF A SECRET

Roger and Lori

The team was aware from the beginning that Lori had decided to leave the marriage after having been romantically involved for two years with her colleague, James. James had already separated from his wife, and he and Lori planned to continue their relationship after her divorce. Roger and Lori had two children, five-year-old Jan and one-year-old Jacob. Both parents told the team they had a goal of sharing both decision-making and time with the children. The full team had met with the clients for the signing of the Participation Agreement. The coaches had had one very difficult meeting with the clients to begin discussing an interim weekly schedule of parenting time. Roger and Lori were unable to come to any agreement on an initial schedule, despite the fact that Lori was quite impatient to move out of the marital home and did not want to do so until an interim schedule was in place. In an individual meeting a few days later, Lori disclosed to Adele, her coach, that she was particularly worried about the weekly schedule because she believed that Jacob was actually the biological child of James, not Roger. Lori knew that James would want to be involved in parenting Jacob in the future, once she separated from Roger. She feared disclosing her suspicion to Roger, but felt that determining Jacob's paternity through a DNA test was essential. Lori felt that the issue of paternity would affect the ultimate time-sharing schedule in some way, but she was not clear how. The issue of Jacob's paternity was clearly going to be emotionally explosive for Roger and for the family going forward. It would have implications for almost every aspect of this case—it was a true land mine.

As we've noted, if the land mine issue is the necessary disclosure of a secret, the sequencing of discussions related to it is important. For example, in cases in which a coach learns from his client of an ongoing affair, a new boyfriend, or a hidden financial factor, the coach will want to let the other team members know that a secret has been shared and that the client will soon be prepared to talk about this with the spouse. However, the rest of the team may not feel comfortable hearing the content of the secret before the other spouse does. If the secret and all of its intricacies are given to the spouse's attorney and/or coach, that in turn may create a situation in which the spouse's own team must carry the secret for a period of time. Learning later that a team held information to which one client was not privy can be very upsetting for that client—who has, after all, placed his or her trust in the team to support the ideal of transparency on germane issues.

Consider the case of Roger and Lori above. When Adele learned that Lori had questions about her son's paternity, Adele had to decide who on the team should be told and in what sequence. She quickly realized how unfair and humiliating the situation could be for Roger, who could become the last of many people to learn that his son might not be his biological child. Adele needed to think through the implications, for Roger's own coach and attorney, of holding this information—even for several hours or days prior to their client receiving the news. On the other hand, without being able to talk through how to navigate this minefield with her teammates, Adele was left feeling overwhelmed and uncertain.

The crucial point is that the professional who first learns of any information that could be acutely distressing, surprising, or threatening for the other client should tread carefully. Talking first with the other professional on your "side" of the team might make sense (e.g., a coach talking first with her client's attorney). Maybe talking coach to coach or attorney to attorney might feel safest. Alternatively, talking with everyone on the team in *general* terms might be the best way forward. It's not that there is one right path with specific steps you *must* follow. The crucial tactic is to thoughtfully consider the future before taking action. Remember: just because you happened to be the unfortunate soul who caught the grenade doesn't mean you need to pull the pin. Despite the predictable anxiety you will feel if the issue lands in your lap first, give yourself permission to take a breath, take your time, consider whom on your team to talk to next, and think together about how to proceed in your coordination and planning.

Once we have consulted with our teammates and walked through the steps of the CLASP model, we will have a sense of whether and

> "Remember: just because you happened to be the unfortunate soul who caught the grenade doesn't mean you need to pull the pin. Despite the predictable anxiety you will feel if the issue lands in your lap first, give yourself permission to take a breath, take your time, and consider whom on your team to talk to next, and think together about how to proceed in your coordination and planning."

how to help one client disclose the essential information to the other. We will then need preparatory meetings with each client and his or her attorney and/or coach. Before asking a client to disclose any sensitive and surprising information, we need to help prepare both clients for the potential emotional fallout of the disclosure and for any concrete implications.

One thing we will be thinking about when we talk with our clients is how each client prefers to manage the moment of disclosure—in a four-way talk with the coaches, in a full team meeting, or perhaps through a letter followed up with a face-to-face meeting. We will also want to explore whether either client prefers that some information about the secret be delivered ahead of time to the receiver of the news—perhaps by their coach or attorney. Sometimes people prefer to be able to feel the first punch of information in relative privacy, or in the relatively safe space of their own professionals' offices. Again: there is no one right way to prepare clients for an explosive disclosure. The decisions about how to set up the disclosure discussion will depend on input from both clients, as well as on the thoughts of the professionals who are working with them.

▼▼▼▼▼

Preparatory Meeting with Client Who Will Disclose Potentially Explosive Information: A Hypothetical Agenda

- Review the information to be disclosed.
- Help the disclosing client decide how much/which information to share.
- Discuss potential settings for disclosure and who might be present (coaches? attorneys? full team?).
- Discuss potential timing of disclosure (the sooner the better? If not, why not?).
- Help the client to anticipate his or her spouse's potential reactions to the disclosure.

- Help the client to anticipate his or her own emotions during the disclosure.
- Help the client to explore possible long-term emotional implications of the disclosure for the family.
- Help the client to explore possible long-term concrete implications for the family.
- Role play the moment of disclosure to prepare the client to articulate information effectively and to decrease his or her anxiety.
- Offer guidance to the client about ways to remain respectful, genuine, and kind.
- Reference the clients' Mission Statement and help him or her remain focused on the children and/or important goals for the future.
- Strategize with the client about what to do if he or she becomes emotionally overwhelmed during the disclosure, if his or her spouse becomes overwhelmed, or if conversation becomes distressing.

▼▼▼▼▼

Preparatory Meeting with the Client Who Will Be Receiving the Information: A Hypothetical Agenda

- Review a basic outline of information to be shared.
- Discuss how much detail the client wants to hear.
- Explore the ramifications of hearing more or fewer details.
- Discuss potential settings for the disclosure and who might be present.
- Discuss potential timing of the disclosure.
- Help the client to anticipate his or her reactions to hearing the information.
- Help the client to anticipate the long-term impact of learning the information (if the substance of the information is known in advance of the disclosure).

- Help the client to develop plans for short-term strategies for managing the stress and distress of the disclosure *resulting from the meeting.* (Should the client plan to spend the remainder of the day with a trusted friend or family member? Should the client plan for a babysitter for the children after the meeting? Should the client plan to go home after the meeting, rather than back to work?)
- Offer guidance to the client about how to remain relatively composed during the disclosure meeting.
- Reference the client's Mission Statement and help him or her remain focused on the children and/or important goals for the future
- Troubleshoot with the client about what can be done if he or she feels overwhelmed during the meeting and remind the client that you can caucus and take breaks as needed.

HELPING CLIENTS TO TALK TO EACH OTHER ABOUT EXPLOSIVE ISSUES

Remember our discussion of the Macro- and Microcontainers, and the way in which the relationship between the two recapitulates the mother–child relationship? Just as the mother/child dyad requires the support of the mother's partner and extended social network, so does the professional/client dyad (the Microcontainer) require the support of the team (the Macrocontainer) in managing explosive issues. The preparatory and the one-on-one work with clients recalls the work of the competent parent who helps their distraught, frightened, or angry child by providing a safe psychological environment in which the child can tolerate and name the problem, consider various ways of managing it, and tolerate the feelings stirred up as they work it through. The good parent empathizes with but does not take on the child's worries. He or she remains patient and grounded, able to offer containment of anxiety and the hope of successful resolution at a time when the child fears failure, rejection, loss, and humiliation. But as anyone who has ever had to let their infant cry so that the he could learn to self soothe and sleep through the night or has ever had to say a firm good-bye to their tearful nursery-schooler will tell you—even the best parents need support in supporting their children. In fact, it's the best parents who look for support from others when the going gets rough. The same is true of us as Collaborative practitioners. Pulling together as a team and following the CLASP approach will provide an environment in which you can think through complicated scenarios and maintain your emotional equilibrium—even in the face of a land mine.

Once the preparation for a disclosure is done, the actual meeting can take place. The cast of characters for this meeting will depend on the needs and circumstances of the clients; it might include attorneys or coaches only, or it might include the whole team. In Chapter 4, we discussed the techniques we employ in creating a safe Microcontainer. In Chapter 6, we explored the ways in which team functioning can either create or destroy a strong Macrocontainer. Here we will review some of the specific tried-and-true techniques for use in an explosive or potentially explosive meeting:

CLIENT-TO-CLIENT DISCUSSION OF LAND MINE ISSUE

- Provide structure for the discussion.
- Help each client to take turns speaking and listening.
- Help each client to employ emotional strategies reviewed beforehand in order to remain respectful and composed.
- Use caucusing to touch base with your client individually as needed.
- Use time-outs or breaks to help clients collect themselves as needed.
- Check in with each client about how they are feeling at various points during discussion.
- At moments of particular tension or hostile expression, help clients to recall Mission Statement goals, interests of children, and other long-range shared goals.
- When the discussion feels complete, review guidelines for behavior and boundaries following the meeting to ensure the emotional safety of both clients.

- Debrief with your own client immediately following the meeting.

LAND MINE EXAMPLE # 2: A LAND MINE EXPLODED—A CASE THAT COULD FALL OUT

Jessie and Anna

Jessie disclosed to her attorney and coach at the start of the case that she was involved with another woman and knew that Anna had suspicions. Anna confirmed that she believed Jessie was leaving her because of infidelity, but said she did not know with whom Jessie was involved. The couple had adopted twins from China two years previously, and both women initially stated a wish to share parenting time equally.

Though Jessie volunteered the information about her infidelity to her team professionals, she did not explain that she feared telling Anna the identity of her new girlfriend. Leigh, the new woman in Jessie's life, had been a close friend to both clients for years—and in fact had been Anna's college roommate and best friend. Jessie and Leigh planned to stay together in the future, and both feared that the situation would be so upsetting to Anna that she would seek to block their access to the twins. When talking to her attorney and coach, Jessie felt ashamed of her betrayal of Anna with a person particularly dear to Anna, and never told her team the significance of Leigh's place in Anna's life and history.

While the team shared Jessie's concerns about openly discussing her infidelity with Anna, everyone considered the disclosure necessary and inevitable. Everyone hoped that the Collaborative team would be able to help the couple to manage this painful disclosure, and to offer them a way of working through a distressing situation without resorting to an all-out custody battle.

Despite careful preparation of both clients, however, when Anna learned in a four-way meeting with coaches about Jessie's six-month-long relationship with Leigh, she was distraught and abruptly halted the meeting. Although her coach had worked hard with Anna prior to and during the meeting to help her avoid making any quick decisions following the disclosure, Anna decided within hours of the meeting to move out of her home with Jessie and move into her sister's house an hour away. Anna also decided to drive directly to the children's day care center and pick them both up, taking them with her to her sister's home.

In the days following the disclosure, Anna talked about firing her Collaborative attorney and terminating the process. She agreed to meet with her coach, and used that meeting to express her grief and rage. Her coach and attorney spoke with her daily by phone, encouraged her to meet with an individual therapist, and urged her to take some time to process what she had learned before deciding on a course of action. The case had clearly hit a crisis that threatened the process. The question of whether the Collaborative container would ultimately hold these clients in the process would be determined by the clients' capacity to survive the emotional distress of the land mine.

The case of Jessie and Anna highlights a few particular dangers that are common in cases involving land mines. Let's think about those, along with some tips that we've found helpful in managing those dangers.

Whenever we hear about an affair, or a relationship a client has begun since the separation from the spouse, we should assume that the client having the relationship is experiencing some amount of shame, discomfort, or worry about being judged or criticized. The same is true if there is hidden debt or addictive behavior.

> "When a client discloses in an early meeting that he or she has participated in any sort of behavior or relationship that might cause us to raise our eyebrows, we should gently but persistently dig for the entire story."

We've all been in the position of having to "'fess up" and have struggled with our own guilt and worried about being vilified. What do we do in the face of those feelings? On our better days, we deal with our transgressions honestly and straightforwardly. More typically, though, we minimize dirty details in an attempt to protect both ourselves and the recipients of our confession.

So when a client discloses in an early meeting that he or she has participated in any sort of behavior or relationship that might cause us to raise our eyebrows, we should gently but persistently dig for the entire story. We can remind our client of the importance

of full disclosure and mutual trust. We can help our client to anticipate the potential risks of not disclosing fully (and sooner rather
than later). We can also offer our client reassurance, support, and
the promise of our compassion.

In the case of Jessie and Anna, the team professionals did their
due diligence in exploring what they perceived as the potential
land mine at the start of the case—the affair. Jessie's attorney and
coach knew enough to explore the issue of Jessie's relationship
with Leigh, but it never occurred to either of them to explore the
critical issue that Jessie had not brought into the discussion—the matter of Leigh's preexisting relationship to the
couple. Perhaps if they had done so, the trajectory of the
case might have been differ-ent. Perhaps, armed with the
full story, Anna's team could have emotionally prepared

> "We should assume that clients will sometimes withhold details of their stories in an attempt at self-protection, and we should maintain an inquiring stance. In Collaborative Practice, as in life, it's the unknown, not the known, that is the most dangerous."

her for the disclosure in such a way that she could have more easily
remained in the process. Perhaps not. We can never think of every
question to ask, nor shine a light in every dark corner of our client's
story. Ultimately the choice of what to disclose and what to hold
back, whether it's made consciously or unconsciously, is that of
our client. Still, we should assume that clients will sometimes with-
hold details of their stories in an attempt at self-protection, and we
should maintain an inquiring stance. In Collaborative Practice, as in
life, it's the unknown, not the known, that is the most dangerous.

FACTORS THAT MIGHT DETERMINE
IF A LAND MINE WILL END A CASE

Anna's immediate reaction to learning about Leigh and Jessie is
understandable, even predictable. It may take her months or years
to fully recover from the betrayal. But if, over time, Anna is able
to refind some positive feelings about Jessie, if those feelings can
coexist in Anna's mind along with her grief and anger, she may

▼

"One critical factor that determines whether a land mine will be a transitory crisis or a Collaborative death knell is the psychological health or ill-health—the flexibility or rigidity—of the person receiving the upsetting information. . . . Another critical factor is the health of the disclosing client."

be able to move into a productive co-parenting relationship with her former partner. One critical factor that determines whether a land mine will be a transitory crisis or a Collaborative death knell is the psychological health or ill-health—the flexibility or rigidity—of the person receiving the upsetting information.

If Anna is fragile and vulnerable to splitting, if she quickly and intractably moves to seeing Jessie as a persecutor and to revenge as her only option, termination is a likely outcome.

Another critical factor is the health of the disclosing client. If Jessie is patient with Anna, expresses sincere remorse for hurting her, and gives her plenty of time to recover, Anna's ability to return to the Collaborative table might be bolstered. As we have noted, couples live within a relationship dynamic and their dance is a duet. If Anna can recognize her own contributions to the unhappiness in the marriage (if she can see she is a "Lock" to Jessie's "Key") she may eventually forgive Jessie, and feel able to reconnect with her as a cooperative co-parent. If she is able to do that before too much time passes, she and Jessie may be able to remain in the Collaborative process.

SUMMARY

Thematic difficulties flow through every Collaborative case, raising tension and triggering conflicts. Some cases also include specific, highly provocative issues that may or may not be anticipated by team members. These highly charged issues have the capacity to derail the communication of the team and threaten both the Micro- and Macrocontainers—the relationships between each and every person on the team and both clients. We have called these issues land mines, because of their explosive nature and because many issues in this category tend to be hidden from view for a time. What we have learned from our work is that there are a few crucial concepts to bear in mind as you set off on your journey through any Collaborative case. Adherence to these concepts can potentially prevent profound damage to either of the clients and help you to keep your case alive. They are as follows:

- Take your time—don't panic!
- When the going gets rough, hold on to your team: remember the CLASP approach.
- Remain alert to your own feelings, triggers, and countertransferences.
- Be mindful of your client's dynamics, the couple's dynamics, and how those patterns may be playing out in the case.
- Make use of your insights about your clients to develop a deeper understanding of how to help them.
- Use both the Microcontainers and the Macrocontainer to help guide your clients through to safety.

▼▼▼▼▼

Regression at the Eleventh Hour: Not Necessarily a Land Mine

Consider two scenarios:

- After six months of hard work, your clients are finally ready to sign a carefully crafted Agreement. At 10 p.m. on the night before your final meeting, you receive an e-mail from your client: "I spoke to my brother. He thinks I shouldn't sell the house after all. I need to rethink everything."

- Your client came to you as a grieving and angry wife who, even though her husband left her in order to pursue a relationship with her best friend, was initially desperate to hold on to her marriage. In early meetings, even though the team was empathic and supportive and her husband was apologetic and generous, she had difficulty moving away from ruminating over the possibility of reconciliation. Over the course of many months, through a combination of support, limit setting, and education, you were able to help her manage her overwhelming anger and grief, develop a nuanced view of her marriage, identify hope for the future, and take an active role in the Collaborative process. Now, in the last 15 minutes of what was to be the last parenting planning meeting, she suddenly blurts out: "You know what, forget this fifty/fifty thing. I don't know what I was thinking. It was his decision to leave me and the kids. What kind of man does that? I want to redo the whole plan."

The above are rather extreme, but not unusual, examples of a phenomenon we frequently experience: just as clients approach the signing of a Collaborative Agreement, one or both of them regresses to earlier positions or ways of relating to their spouse or to the team. Sometimes, they even threaten to "pull the plug"; we've had many clients question whether the Collaborative process is "right" for them after all, even as the other party waits for them to put pen to paper. What to make of this? What to do?

We understand the creation of last minute "crises" as a natural response to the feelings stirred up in our clients by the sense of finality associated with the end of an important phase in their divorce. The close of the formal portion of the Collaborative process can stimulate old emotions, or, for clients who have been in denial, can catalyze a new awareness of the import of their decisions. Because of the intensity of feeling driving regressive behaviors, and because (as in the above examples) they often have dramatic content, it takes self-restraint on the part of team members not to panic or move quickly into action.

What we find, though, is that if we simply take a breath and see these regressions in context, we can keep our Collaborative process intact. In virtually every case in which our clients appeared to want to turn things upside down at the last minute, we have found that we could bring them back from the brink by saying something like: "You know, coming to the end of the process is really a big deal; it means your divorce is real. We find that people often second-guess themselves and each other at this stage, because letting go means accepting that your life is changing. Even though you may feel divorce is really the right way to go, it's still sad. You can go forward feeling you've made a good Agreement, but that doesn't mean you haven't suffered terrible losses."

It's worth noting that we find the "eleventh hour regression" so common that we now help clients to anticipate it. Somewhere toward the end of the process we prepare them by helping them to understand that, as we reach Agreement, they will likely experience a resurgence or intensifying of painful feelings. This intervention normalizes our clients' experience and, while it may not prevent last-minute disruptions, it will likely help the team to support the clients in weathering their emotional storm without behaving destructively.

The Voice of the Child: The Crucial Role of the Child Specialist

8

The Added Value of the Child Specialist

One way the Collaborative model is distinctly different from other methods of resolving legal disputes arising from divorce is that it invites the voices of the children to be heard and addressed in sensitive and useful ways. The careful manner in which we handle our direct communication with the children allows us to think about difficulties in the relationship of the children to one or both parents with an eye toward shoring up these relationships, rather than as part of an attempt by one side to garner ammunition for use against the other (as in traditional negotiation). In the Collaborative model we care about children's feelings and wishes, we rely on their insights, and we shine a light on their experience. But we don't put children in the middle of parental disputes, nor ask them to choose sides.

It might not surprise you to learn that very few parents discuss their separation with their children in advance of its happening, and even fewer consult their children as they plan for their post-separation future. It has certainly been our experience that our clients, overwhelmed by their own emotional experience as their marriage ends, often lose sight of the impact of their decisions on their children. Even though most parents care deeply about their kids and want to keep their kids' needs front and center (many have read books on helping children through divorce, and others ask for references), in practice parents often have difficulty separating their own feelings from those of their children. The result is that children often feel alone and abandoned, with a sense that their parents do not recognize that they have a separate emotional reality. In addition to grief, shock, anger, and guilt (the gamut of expectable feelings), children in this situation often feel powerless and disenfranchised.

The Collaborative child specialist steps into the eye of the emotional storm. He or she metaphorically takes each parent by the hand, offering the message "I am here to help, not to judge or criticize. You know your child best, and I respect that. But because I am a professional with knowledge and experience in both child development and divorce, I will be able to help you and your team think about how to plan best for your children." He or she also metaphorically takes each child by the hand, offering the message: "I know this is a really scary and upsetting time. Your parents know this too, and that's why we're here together. Tell me how you're doing, what kinds of questions you have, and anything you'd like your parents to know. Though I'll be talking with your parents later, this is a safe place. You are not here because you are in trouble. You're here because your parents would like to better understand you and how to plan for your family going forward."

Child specialists typically begin their work by meeting individually with each parent once or twice. This gives the professional a chance to hear each parent's story, identify concerns and questions, and get a beginning sense of each parent's personality organization. Equally importantly, the child specialist is working to develop the Microcontainer of his or her relationship with each parent, a strong working alliance that will allow each parent to hear whatever the child specialist has to offer at a later meeting.

Child specialists then move into meeting with the child or children. If there is more than one sibling, the professional will usually meet with each child alone as well as in their sibling group. Again, the child specialist works to develop a strong Microcontainer. Some child specialists work in the children's own home or homes, while others meet in a therapeutic playroom or office. The sessions are designed to make the children feel comfortable and relaxed. While some parents worry that their children will experience these sessions as anxiety-producing or intrusive, we find that the reverse is true. Children very quickly and easily grasp the child specialist's role, and almost universally experience the meetings as a welcome relief.

Through talk and play, the child specialist works with the children to figure out what important messages the professional should carry back to the parents and what messages the children would like to deliver to their parents directly. Together, the child specialist and the children might work to craft language for this communication. The children might also begin to identify information that they'd like the child specialist to know and remember but not yet share with their parents. This joint decision-making about the form and timing of information-sharing (and the explorations of underlying concerns) is itself empowering and new for many kids. Suddenly, their opinions are valued. They are being invited into an important adult discussion (sometimes for the first time), but in ways that feel safe. The grown-ups will listen, but the parents will still be parents and make decisions about how best to integrate their children's thoughts and feelings.

Once the child specialist has completed the "data collection" phase of the work, he or she typically has a debrief call with the mental health members of the team (or attorneys if there are no coaches). The three professionals then schedule a meeting with the parents. Parents often enter the room feeling worried that their parenting will come under attack. However, even if the child specialist has painful information to convey, parents usually relax when they find that this information is shared in a spirit of supportive concern. This is a very special sort of discussion, and parents listen closely and intensely. The child specialist talks to the parents about their children without making concrete recommendations about custody or time, focusing instead on some of the essential aspects of the children's current experience and how that experience might inform the parents' plans. Because the child specialist is careful to say that he or she will not generate a written report, the information flows in a conversation, with give and take between the parents and the professionals. Powerful emotions often surface during this meeting, and they are recognized and respected. But professionals work to keep the needs of the children as the central focus. Because the child specialist is neutral, and working apart from the complicated interactions of the rest of the team, this aspect of the work is uniquely cushioned from the rest of the Collaborative process. And that's a good thing, because it is also uniquely essential.

But let's not forget the importance of the Macrocontainer. The team will be interested in the child specialist's thoughts about the children, and dedicated to helping both parents make use of this feedback to create the best parenting plan possible. Interestingly, we have noticed that many tense junctures during financial meetings have hinged on the team's recollection of a piece of information gained about the children from the child specialist. When a team has the presence of mind to link insight offered by the child specialist to some aspect of the clients' Mission Statement in order to bring the clients' shared parenting goals back into focus, impasses can be broken and brainstorming can be infused with new energy. Recalled in the context of the family's ongoing work, the words of the child specialist take on renewed and more powerful meaning.

THE IMPORTANCE OF THE CHILD'S VOICE: A VIGNETTE

Bill and Janet had one son, 10-year-old Charlie. After years of marital distress, Bill had disclosed to Janet that he was gay. He loved Janet, but could no longer tolerate living a lie. Charlie had a wonderful relationship with each parent, and both parents were very involved in his life. Bill and Janet separated just as they entered the Collaborative process, and were already living apart when they first met Ellen, the child specialist their team had recommended. While Charlie obvi-

ously knew his dad had moved into a townhouse, neither parent had yet told him of their plan to get divorced, nor mentioned anything about the reasons. They had simply said, "We need to have some time apart, and you are going to spend some time at Dad's house, and some time here with Mom."

Bill was impatient to explain the situation fully to Charlie. Janet felt worried about "burdening" Charlie with grown-up information. She felt he should be given time to "adapt to all the changes" before being told about the divorce and his father's sexual orientation. While there was not much conflict between the parents about the parenting schedule with Charlie, the issue of what to tell Charlie, and when, was creating quite a bit of friction between them.

Ellen met with the parents together, which was their preference. They both spoke animatedly about their son. Bill and Janet's distress surfaced only when talking about what to tell Charlie, as if the reality of the changes in their lives was only truly felt when thinking about how to put it all into words. Janet seemed to feel that as long as the truth wasn't spoken to Charlie, the upsetting reality might change.

Ellen met with Charlie in her office, which was lined with shelves stacked with board games, containers of toys, a doll house, a castle inhabited by small plastic knights, and a cannon that fired plastic cannon balls at the push of a tiny button. Charlie immediately got to work setting up knights in a line in front of the castle, shooting cannon balls, and knocking down all the knights. As he played, he and Ellen chatted about the recent events in his life. When they got to talking about the "best" and "worst" things about each of his homes, Charlie made a surprising comment. "Well, you know it doesn't really matter that my Dad doesn't have a Wii because pretty soon we'll all be back at the big house." Ellen asked what he meant. "My mom and dad just need time apart," he replied. "I think they are waiting for me to decide when they have had enough time, and when they are in good moods again. When I can tell they are both pretty happy, I will let them know it's time for Dad to come home." Ellen replied, "So you are thinking this might be your decision, huh? About when the family should live together again?" "Oh yeah," Charlie answered, his voice quavering a bit. "The only problem is, I'm not sure how I will know when it's been long enough. How do you think I will figure out when Dad can come home?"

Ellen talked through this quandary with Charlie, helping him to consider the possibility that his parents had decided to live separately for reasons having nothing to do with him, and that perhaps he did not actually have responsibility for making these decisions (though part of him might wish he did). Charlie remained steadfast, though, in his belief that the job of reconciling his parents was somehow his to complete.

Ellen spent two sessions with Charlie, in which he played with the castle, drew pictures of his family and his two houses, and talked about various aspects of his life. Charlie seemed to be a confident child, and comfortable with each parent when they brought him in to see Ellen. However, Ellen noticed that his voice broke and his cheeks turned bright red when he talked about the upcoming holidays, when he recalled his parents telling him about his dad's new home, and when he spoke again about his looming "big decision"—how and when to bring his parents together again.

Ellen met again with Bill and Janet, this time with both of their coaches (who had been briefed, along with the rest of the team, in a team conference call shortly before the five-way meeting). Ellen began by telling Bill and Janet what a neat kid Charlie was, and how much she had enjoyed spending a little time with him. Ellen then began to talk about her two sessions with Charlie and all she had learned. She reassured Bill and Janet that Charlie seemed generally healthy and resilient, but said that he was also sad and very worried. Both parents' eyes filled with tears at this. Ellen explained about Charlie's sense of responsibility for his family's future, and his belief (both a worry and a fantasy!) that he had control over when it was time for his dad to come home.

Ellen said, "I know neither of you said anything like this to Charlie. Children tend to feel they are at the center of everything as a matter of course. This is both a common wish and a fear for all children. Charlie is trying to be 'grown up' about all the changes, but he is worried about how he's supposed to fix the problems. Of course, part of Charlie also wants to believe he has that power." Janet began to cry. "I had no idea. I had no idea," she said. Bill reached his hand out and patted Janet's knee. "Of course you didn't, Jan. Neither did I. How could we? He never said a word about this. And we didn't know to ask."

The rest of the conversation with Ellen went smoothly. Ellen, with the help of the coaches, helped Bill and Janet discuss the development of a shared narrative—an explanation for Charlie about what was happening in his family and why. Both parents voiced their mutual wish to relieve their son of his sense of responsibility and to help him understand and accept what the family's future might look like. Both parents said that they wanted to sit down with Charlie over the coming weekend to talk about the upcoming divorce and to talk about Bill's sexual identity in a way that Charlie could understand. Both parents realized how important it would be for Charlie to feel comfortable asking either parent questions as time went on.

The coaches promised both clients that they would continue to work on the parenting plan with them after this meeting, and that they would all be able to call on Ellen as a resource if questions came up. Months later, when Bill and Janet signed their Divorce Agreement, both noted to their attorneys that they would feel eternally grateful to Ellen—with whom they had met a total of four times. "Ellen really got Charlie talking, and he really liked her. Thank goodness she helped us understand what he was thinking back then," Bill said. Janet added, "I hate to think what our lives would be like right now—what Charlie's life would be like right now—if Charlie hadn't met with Ellen. He might still be trying to take care of us, and we wouldn't be taking such good care of him."

▼▼▼▼▼

The Role of the Child Specialist: Some Key Points*

- A child specialist is a collaboratively trained mental health professional with extensive experience in child development, family dynamics, and separation and divorce.

* We have described the role of the child specialist in the way that we use it in practice—as a neutral on a team that includes other mental health professionals. We recognize that other professionals conceptualize the role differently. For example, some teams utilize a sole mental health neutral who performs the role of coach and child specialist, while on other teams it is the child specialist (not the coaches) who helps the parents to develop a parenting plan.

- A child specialist is most useful when brought into the case from the start, but can be helpful at any point in the parenting planning process (especially when parents feel the need).
- A child specialist helps to increase parents' awareness of children's autonomous feelings, wishes, fears, and needs.
- A child specialist helps parents to support each other as co-parents, rather than use perceived vulnerabilities in the other as "ammunition."
- A child specialist helps to educate parents about the way children cognitively process separation and divorce.
- A child specialist helps to educate parents about what children may need in an access schedule at different developmental stages.
- A child specialist may offer recommendations as to how the parents can help their children cope with sadness, grief, anger, and worry.
- A child specialist, along with other team members, can offer referrals to other professionals as needed (e.g., child therapist, learning specialists). Note: Parents should understand, from the beginning, that the child specialist will not be able to change roles in order to provide psychotherapy to any family member in the future.
- A child specialist will remain available throughout the Collaborative process and after as needed (e.g., to offer a "check-in" with children after some period of time).

Developing a Deep and Durable Parenting Plan*   9

A "Custody Agreement" versus a "Parenting Plan"

Traditional models of divorce rely on the creation of a legal document called a "Custody and Visitation Agreement." This tends to be a dry and impersonal contract that mandates logistical behaviors, decision-making, and the division of the children's time. Even the title of the document implies an emphasis on the legal rights of one parent to have control over the children. The description of the analogous document in Collaborative Practice as a "parenting plan" is purposeful. We want parents to feel as much ownership of this part of their Agreement as of any other part. The parenting plan will eventually become part of a legal contract. But it will be a document that reflects the recognition that though they will not longer be a romantic couple, they will remain a parenting couple.

---

* We were introduced to the phrase "deep and durable" when we heard Pauline Tesler and Peggy Thompson use it in a training program that we attended in April 2009. We love it and have used it liberally ever since. We're grateful to them.

The parenting plan will represent their vision of a reconstituted family. It will emerge from a carefully considered definition of a new co-parenting relationship, and will represent a shared vision for raising their children into adulthood.

All of us who have worked with separating parents over the years are familiar with the standard checklist of issues, or "clauses," that parents generally need to discuss when creating a thorough parenting plan. We know that some plans are quite detailed, with, for example, careful attention to exact times and days of transitions of the children and intricate descriptions of how the holidays will be shared. Other plans are more basic, referring repeatedly to the parents' agreement "to reach a mutually satisfying arrangement through discussion" prior to a holiday or special event, without spelling out what that arrangement will be. Parenting plans can be tailored to fit a family's emotional culture and the abilities of particular parents to negotiate and compromise spontaneously.

EVERY PLAN HAS ITS OWN "FLAVOR"

Every parenting plan develops its own theme, or what we like to call "flavor," created by the complexity of ingredients each parent contributes. These ingredients include their personalities, belief systems, values, capacity for insight, and self-awareness. After working with one couple for a meeting or two, you might begin to notice that both parents tend to avoid working too long on any issue, preferring to jump quickly to what is "simple." Their plan may develop a "loose" flavor that is heavy on cooperative spirit but light on detail or forethought. In working with another couple, you might recognize that they consider each issue, no matter how trivial, in minute detail—looking at it from every conceivable angle and trying to anticipate any potential eventuality. Their plan may take on a flavor

> "Every parenting plan develops its own theme, or what we like to call 'flavor,' created by the complexity of ingredients each parent contributes. These ingredients include their personalities, belief systems, values, capacity for insight, and self-awareness."

of micromanagement, with rules for how they will handle even the smallest details of co-parenting. In our toughest cases, the parents have dichotomous styles. Perhaps Mom is the one who wants to look at every clause in the parenting plan under a microscope, while Dad—who prefers to live "in the moment"—would rather they plan to make decisions about their kids "on the fly." Parents with differing styles are likely to come to the process already feeling

mutually provoked, angry, and unsympathetic. Helping these folks to craft a mutually agreeable parenting plan will be arduous, as you will all need to find a way to balance contrasting flavors in an integrated way in order to satisfy the needs of each.

If you now find yourself thinking back to our earlier discussion of the Lock and Key, you're getting the picture. All of our clients bring their marital dynamic to the parenting planning work. As we guide them through this phase, we hope to help each couple redefine their relationship in ways that will enable them to avoid reenacting their marital dynamic over time, or, as we sometimes like to say to parents, "recreating their marriage in their divorce."

If we recall what we know about the Rigidity/Flexibility Continuum, we can immediately see how our clients' functioning in the parenting arena will be influenced by their more general strengths and vulnerabilities. When you're faced with a parent who insists on telling the children that his wife is "leaving us because she wants to be with her lover," think about the underlying rigidity of that stance. When you note the willingness of parents to forgo long vacations in order to prevent long separations of either of them from their toddler, recall the idea of flexibility and its implications for empathy and mature planning.

THE RIGIDITY/FLEXIBILITY CONTINUUM APPLIED TO CO-PARENTING

Rigid ⟷ Flexible

Narcissistic parenting positions ⟷ Focused on best interest of child

Acts out marital wounds ⟷ Able to separate marital wounds from parenting style and decision-making

Distorted sense of own and other's parenting capacities/fitness ⟷ Realistic sense of own and other's parenting capacities/fitness

Unable to tolerate differences in style/approach in co-parent ⟷ Able to tolerate differences in style/approach in co-parent

Closed to input from ⟷ Open to input from professionals
professionals and   and co-parent
co-parent

Indifferent to co-parent's ⟷ Empathic toward co-parent's
feelings   feelings

If you haven't yet done many parenting plans in your professional work, you might feel anxious moving into this part of the process. The actual building blocks of the parenting plans (e.g., the division of holidays, the weekly access plan) and the typical range of options for dealing with them are easy to learn (and we've briefly discussed them below). There are lots of good books on the subject, and we suggest, if you haven't done so already, that you find an IACP-approved training program that reviews those nuts and bolts. The answers to such questions as "What is the best access schedule for an 18-month-old?" or "What are some ways that parents can divide treasured holidays?" are important and interesting, but outside the scope of this book. Our focus is the process of understanding and navigating a couple's emotional dynamic. The rest of this chapter will apply all of the concepts we have already explored to the construction of the parenting plan.

▼▼▼▼▼

Typical Building Blocks of a Collaborative Parenting Plan

Mission Statement

A Mission Statement can consist of either bullet points or prose that captures the shared goals and aspirations of the parents for their children into the future. The Mission Statement can also include goals and aspirations related to achieving a healthy co-parenting relationship.

Shared Narrative

This is the term the authors have coined to describe the story that parents jointly develop, usually with the help of the Collaborative professionals, to explain their divorce to their children. Sometimes parents develop secondary and tertiary narratives for use with extended family, friends, and their larger community.

Weekly Access Schedule

Weekly access schedules describe where the children are routinely going to be each week. The weekly schedule should include where the children will spend both daytime hours and overnights, and discuss how the parents will transition the children from place to place.

Decision Making

- Education
- Health
- Mental health
- Religion
- Extracurricular activities
- Miscellaneous

Summer

- Vacations
- Weekly schedule, if at all different from schedule during school year
- Protocols for planning children's summer activities, such as sleep-away or day camps

Major Holidays/School Breaks

- Thanksgiving
- Winter break and winter holidays, such as Christmas, Hannukah, Kwanza
- Spring break
- Specific religious holidays, such as Yom Kippur, Easter
- One-day federal holidays (Labor Day, Columbus Day, Veteran's Day, Martin Luther King Day, Presidents' Day, Memorial Day, 4th of July)

Scheduled and Unscheduled School Closings
- Parent/teacher conference days
- Teacher training days
- Snow days
- Sick days

Special Days
- Mother's Day and Father's Day
- Birthdays—children's and parents'

Travel Issues
- Protocols for parental communication about upcoming travel plans
- Protocols for parental communication about specific itineraries
- Protocols for communication with children during periods of travel

Relocation
- Do the parents want to designate a geographical region out of which they will not relocate with the children

Right of First Refusal
- Protocols for relying on co-parent instead of alternate care-giver when custodial parent cannot care for children on his or her own scheduled time

Makeup Time
- Protocols determining whether and how parents will arrange make-up time for a parent who misses regularly scheduled time with the children

Communication Protocols
- Protocols for routine communication about the children—rhythm and methods (e.g., e-mail, phone calls, Co-Parenting Log)
- Protocols for routine communication with the children

Dispute-Resolution Protocols

• Discussion of the distinction between a decision about which one parent must (or may) *advise* the other and a decision about which one must *consult* the other
• Protocols for communication about disagreements and co-parenting problems
• Protocols for seeking a third party facilitator, mediator, or a return to the Collaborative process if parents cannot resolve a parenting dispute

Introduction of New Significant Others

• Guidelines for balancing a parent's dating life with protecting the emotional best interests of the children
• Guidelines for communicating with a co-parent about introducing a romantic partner to the children
• Guidelines for how and when to begin integrating a new romantic partner into one's time with the children

▼▼▼▼▼
Developing a Parenting Plan: The Balancing Act

Good parenting planning, like good parenting, is an artful balance between action and restraint. It's not a static balance, but a shifting one—a movement back and forth along a continuum according to an ongoing assessment of your clients' shifting needs. Consider how, in working with your clients, you might hold and address the following manifestations of this tension between doing and not-doing:

• Holding back in order to allow clients to work through anxieties and uncertainties toward reaching a mutual resolution *versus* offering guidance and information
• Offering expert opinion *versus* letting clients reach their own conclusions
• Intervening when you have professional concerns *versus* making way for clients' needs for self-determination

- Looking out for the best interests of the children *versus* pressuring the parents to do something they are unable to do (either for emotional or practical reasons)
- Helping to move the process along efficiently *versus* pushing clients too quickly

PARENTING PLANNING MEETINGS: NAVIGATING THE EMOTIONAL DYNAMICS IN THE ROOM

We are now going to introduce you to some of the most common challenges that crop up in helping clients with their parenting plan. We will take a look at how these challenges relate to the clients' functioning on the Rigidity/Flexibility Continuum, what balancing act the scenario may require from the professionals, and how we the authors might handle these scenarios.

We know that on some teams attorneys will be working on the parenting plan with their clients, while on other teams coaches will be conducting this piece of the work. Some Collaborative communities include mental health professionals trained as child specialists, while others do not. Since we are mental health professionals, our scenarios will include two coaches. Keep in mind that the professionals at the table could just as easily be two attorneys.

We also want to note that some components of the parenting plan (especially the weekly schedule) often take several meetings to address. The passage of time during a case can be crucial for some clients, in that it allows them to slowly adapt to the highly charged notion of time away from their children, work further on their emotional acceptance of the divorce, develop their outside support network, sometimes enter psychotherapy, and gradually become ready to address highly challenging issues such as where their children will sleep each night. Our illustrations here are condensed versions of the process. We know that such brief conversations would typically not advance the work so successfully. A more typical trajectory for resolving the issues illustrated below would include several team meetings, a few phone calls, and an individual meeting or two over a few weeks or months.

SCENARIO 1: A SHARED NARRATIVE CHALLENGE

Terasita and Juan

Terasita had an affair during their marriage. Juan is hurt and angry. Terasita has expressed regret for hurting Juan, feels ashamed of her infidelity, and has decided to get divorced despite having broken off her other relationship. She is able to acknowledge Juan's anger and pain, and she has said that she is willing to accept Juan's wish to tell the children that the divorce is "her fault." However, she is concerned about what information might be most helpful for their daughters, ages 11 and 13, and she has asked the coaches to talk about how to craft an appropriate shared narrative. Juan wants to make sure the children know that he had no part in the marital problems. He feels they should know about their mother's infidelity so that they will be less likely to commit adultery in their future marriages. But he loves his girls, and is worried about how they will react to the coming separation and divorce.

The Four-Way Meeting

[Kate is Terasita's coach, Lisa is Juan's coach]

Lisa: *This is obviously really painful for both of you. I know being honest and up front is important to you both—and it sounds like you are both very concerned about how Lily and Angela will cope with all this difficult news.*

Juan: *Obviously. Yes. I wish Terasita had thought about that before she slept with her boss.*

Terasita: *I've apologized a hundred times, Juan. This needs to be about our girls—not about you or me.*

Lisa: *Based on what I've learned about you in our past conversations, Juan, I think you agree with what Terasita is saying about focusing on your girls—I know how much you care about them.*

Juan: [Choking up a bit, but clearly angry] *Of course I do.*

Lisa: So when you are both talking to Lily and Angela, trying to help them understand why Terasita is moving out, it sounds like there are some things that the two of you might be able to say to your girls that are authentically true for both of you. There may be other things that one or both of you won't be able to say without feeling you are being dishonest. Maybe we can try to focus on the areas that overlap—what you can both feel comfortable saying to the girls that will give them the information they need while protecting them as much as possible from unnecessary pain.

Juan: Okay. Like what?

Lisa: Kate—do you want to talk about that?

Kate: Well, Lisa and I feel that the most important information to give your kids is that you have decided you're not going to be married anymore, which means you won't live together any longer. Let them know this decision was a "grown-up" decision; the girls didn't do anything to cause it and they can't do anything to stop it.

Terasita: You mean, tell them they are not to blame.

Kate: Right. All kids tend to worry that somehow they are the cause of the troubles, and think—hope, really—that they might be able to fix the problems if they stop fighting among themselves, or get better grades—things like that.

Juan: Well, I think telling them their mother is to blame makes sense then. They will know it wasn't their fault.

Lisa: Let's think about that. How do you think Lily and Angela might feel if they come to believe the divorce is their mom's fault?

Juan: They'll be angry, I think—and they will know I didn't want this to happen.

Kate: Juan, could you help us understand why it is important to you that the girls know you did not want this to happen?

Juan: [tearful and angry] The girls are very close to Terry. The three of them do everything together. If they think this is my fault, they'll be mad at me. I don't deserve that!

Terasita: [tearful] Juan, I don't want them to be mad at you—or at me. I want them to know we both love them and will be there for them!

Lisa: One thing Kate and I talk to parents about each time we discuss the shared narrative is the fact that all kids identify with both their parents. They feel they are partly like their moms, and partly like their dads. And in Lily and Angela's case, while they are very close to their mom, they also clearly adore their dad. Juan, you told us how much they love cooking with you and how you taught Lily to barbecue last summer. I don't actually think it would be helpful for either girl to be encouraged to blame either of you. In fact, it would be painful and confusing if they were pushed to see their mom as having betrayed you, Juan. Kate, is this making sense to you? Have other thoughts?

Kate: I agree with everything you've said, Lisa. I would add that if you portray yourself as a victim, Juan, I'd worry that your girls might begin to feel protectively toward you. Then they might not feel free to share all their feelings about what's happening—not just sadness and worry, but anger, too. They'll do best if they feel you're both open and sturdy enough to respond to their whole range of reactions. And it'll help you to feel closer to them, something you've said you're worried about.

Juan: Well, then how do we explain it? What if they ask why we can't stay together?

Kate: I guess it's hard for you to imagine how to answer this question without talking about Terry's affair. The truth is, your children may always push for more information than you feel able or comfortable to give them. The main thing is to acknowledge how upsetting and confusing your decision to divorce is for everyone. For now, it's probably fine to say that while there are some parts of this decision that are really between you and their mom, you want the girls to know that the two of you have thought about this for a long time and have reached the conclusion that you can't be happily married anymore.

Juan: The girls are really smart. I still think they might keep pushing until they get an answer that makes sense.

Lisa: Maybe your worry about this, Juan, is connected to the fact that you still don't feel you have been given an adequate explanation from Terasita about her decision to end the marriage. The feeling that Terry made her decision to leave unilaterally and unfairly is probably something you will need to work on for a while on your own. In the *meantime, can you see the value of speaking to the kids in a way that explains things on their level and leaves lots of space for them to have their own feelings and reactions?*

Juan: [Pause. Coaches do not speak during a rather long silence.] *Yeah. I guess I can.*

THE DEBRIEF

As you read through that transcript, you probably noticed a few of the important issues we were keeping in mind. We wanted to balance our objective of helping Juan to focus more on the interests of his children with an awareness of his need for our empathy and reassurance. Because he was the more fragile (and rigid) of the two parents, we were careful to avoid pushing him too hard or confronting him directly. Lisa, his coach, did most of the heavy lifting in making comments to him, but as the meeting progressed, and he seemed to become somewhat more open to hearing our input, Kate felt it was safe to move in closer. After all, she knew it was important to her own client that she not only play an active role, but also demonstrate an understanding of Juan's difficulty. We tried to weave in information about the children's needs with a recognition and acknowledgement of Juan's pain and point of view, while using his concern for his children to create opportunities to help him let go of his original position.

When Lisa turned to Kate and asked her to comment, both coaches were able to model good parenting—to convey that we were working together on behalf of *both* parents and their children. We found an opportunity to point out how an emotional tension between the spouses (Juan's anger at what he perceived as Terasita's unilateral decision to divorce) might be affecting Juan's parenting decisions. Because he was a relatively brittle, rigid fellow, we didn't hammer the point too hard, but rather left him space to reflect on this dynamic later. We were careful not to say anything that undermined Juan's pride—particularly because we assumed that his wish to blame and punish his wife was a reaction to feeling diminished by her infidelity.

After this meeting, we talked with each other about themes that might resurface as this couple moved through other clauses of their parenting plan. We predicted that Juan's hurt, anger, and desire to punish Terasita would likely flare up repeatedly, particularly at moments he felt she might benefit in some way from the divorce. We anticipated that he might, in certain moments, try to use the parenting plan as a weapon against her. We also wondered if Terasita might be apt to give in to Juan's preferences too quickly, in order to assuage her guilt and avoid Juan's anger. We noted that this pattern of resentment and capitulation was a long-standing marital dynamic between these spouses, and that Terasita's avoidance of conflict with Juan contributed to her seeking an escape hatch from the marriage via her affair. We anticipated that we would have to work hard to help both parents stay focused on the needs of their children. Our concern was that, without our active participation, this parenting plan would take on an overly stringent flavor designed to make Terasita's life harder, accommodate Juan, and minimize the children's needs.

SCENARIO 2: A WEEKLY ACCESS SCHEDULE CHALLENGE

Rashid and Roberta

Rashid has always been the primary breadwinner, working long hours and occasional weekends in a demanding job. Roberta gave up her career when their twins were born; Malik and Cara are now nine years old. In this parenting meeting, Rashid says that he is looking ahead to setting up his own home and wants the chance to get to know his children better. The couple has considerable wealth, and Rashid says he can afford to cut back his hours at work so he can share parenting time with Roberta on a fifty/fifty schedule. Roberta feels enraged that Rashid now—after years of being unavailable to the family—wants to be a fully involved father. She also feels panic-stricken at the idea that she will soon have to be without her twins for some periods of time—especially since she "never wanted this divorce." Roberta has always assumed she would be a full-time mom until the kids went off to college, and has no vision of what she might do with her life if Rashid takes over significant time with their children. When we ask the parents for their thoughts about a weekly schedule, Rashid says he wants to have equal time with the children so they can feel as comfortable and happy in his home as in their mom's. Roberta then says, with considerable emotion, that she strongly believes the kids need to have a primary home. She wants them based with her during each school week. She asserts that "the children are not ping-pong balls," and that she knows children can be severely damaged by being bounced around by their parents.

Lisa and Kate Respond—The First Meeting

[Lisa is Rashid's coach, and Kate is Roberta's coach]

Kate: *Can you say more about that, Roberta? What are you worried about?*

Roberta: *I know lots of kids from divorced homes who have to sleep in one place one night and another place the next. They are not doing well at all.*

Kate: *So one concern you have is that the twins will not adjust well to going back and forth too much.*

Roberta: *Exactly. They need one base where they can feel secure and stable. Don't all kids need that?*

Rashid: *I disagree! I think kids need to have a mother and a father! How are they going to have a father if I see them only every other weekend? That* isn't *going to happen, Roberta.*

Roberta: *Actually, Rashid, I am going to make* sure *it happens. You don't get to call all the shots, you know. Not anymore.*

Lisa: *Okay, so hold up, you guys. Can you tell you're getting into it with each other? Feel familiar?*

Roberta and Rashid: *[mumble, nod]* Yeah.

Lisa: *I'm guessing this is a very scary conversation. The scariest, actually. You're not particularly worried about being financially okay, but each of you has extremely strong feelings about being parents, and about being with Cara and Malik. So even beginning to think about sharing time with them is raising your blood pressure. We aren't even looking at possible options yet.*

Rashid: *It's true. Listen, Roberta. I want you to have plenty of time with the kids—they need you. I know that. I want them to see you a* *lot. But I want to be in their lives too. I don't want to be a Disney dad. I doubt you would want me to be that kind of father either.*

Roberta: [angry] *Don't speak for me, Rashid.*

Lisa: *You know, it occurs to me that you actually had a Disney dad, Rashid, right? Your father traveled a lot, and you pretty much only saw him on special occasions, right?*

Rashid: *Yeah. I basically didn't know him until I was an adult—and then he died when I was 32.*

Lisa: *Roberta, I really get your concern about the kids ping-ponging. You have been on the front lines as a parent for years, and it is truly upsetting to think about being apart from your children. We don't want to minimize what a loss that is. It feels unfair that Rashid is stepping in now, since you feel he hasn't been around for years.*

Roberta: [nods, tears up]

[There is a brief silence in the room, during which both parents seem really sad. Neither coach speaks for a moment.]

Kate: *Roberta, it's clear that you're upset. I think we also sort of dropped Rashid. Rashid, given how painfully you missed your dad when you were little, and how hard it was to lose him after having had so little of him, I think Lisa and I can both appreciate how incredibly important it must feel for you to be close to your children.*

Lisa: *Absolutely. I'm glad you brought us back to that, Kate.*

Kate: *Yeah, I think you and I would agree, Lisa, that no child really wants a Disney dad—all kids need to be close to their fathers, and their mothers.* [Lisa nods supportively] *But this is a tough situation. The kids are used to being with Roberta much of the time. Yet if Rashid can scale back on work, they could really benefit from having more of their dad.*

Lisa: *I am wondering if we should talk more about the idea of including a child specialist in this process, to get input from a neutral expert who could meet you and your kids and offer us some thoughts about their needs.*

Note: We are going to proceed based on the assumption that we have a child specialist available to us. If this were your case and your community does not have a child specialist, or for some reason your team chose not to use one, your discussions with these parents would continue without neutral input. Your work would follow similar paths as ours described below, but you would have less detailed information about the children's needs to call on as you helped Rashid and Roberta explore options. Without the input of the child specialist, your team might have more difficulty helping the parents work through moments of impasse about the children. However, many of the techniques illustrated below could be used even if there had been no child specialist to help out.

Rashid and Roberta have now come to agreement that they will use a child specialist. The child specialist (Sue) spends several weeks meeting with Cara and Malik, talking with each child. She then meets with both parents and their coaches to give them feedback about what she has learned. Sue reports that both kids are very attached to both parents. She says that Malik expresses a yearning to see his dad more, and that both children are healthy, resilient, and adaptable. She suggests that helping the twins, who are in one classroom together, begin to spend some time separate from one another may be helpful to them at this point in their development. They tend to feel anxious when apart, and, at age nine, it would be useful for them to develop some autonomy.

The Next Four-Way Meeting

Kate: *So, having thought about Sue's input, how do each of you feel about going back to our discussion about the weekly schedule?*

Rashid*: I'm ready. I found Sue very helpful. Malik and Cara really liked her.*

Roberta*: I agree, but I did not hear Sue recommending a lot of back-and-forth. So I still feel it would be good to keep the kids at my house during school nights. The summer schedule could be much more flexible.*

Lisa*:* [standing up at the flip chart] *Well, sounds like we might want to start brainstorming some options. Remember, you can come up* *with any idea and I'll write it down. Try not to evaluate yet. Even if you don't like an idea your co-parent suggests, I'll still write it down. We find that doing it this way tends to spark new ideas and help you to feel satisfied that you've explored things fully. But neither of you will be forced to agree to anything you're not comfortable with.*

Roberta: *And I'll have time to think about it, right? I don't have to decide today?*

Kate: *Absolutely. We can even come up with an idea that you and Rashid might want to try out for a few weeks. Then we can come together again to talk about how it went and revisit options. Whatever feels helpful.*

Rashid: *Okay. One idea is that the kids would be with me one week and with Roberta the next. We'll both see them on the weekend at soccer games anyway.*

Lisa: *Okay, that's one option.* [Lisa writes down "Option A: Week-On Week-Off"]

Roberta: [Looking at Rashid as if he is crazy] *You're not serious, Rashid.*

Kate: *I know it's hard to list ideas without evaluating—but these are just options. It's early days yet.*

Roberta: *Okay. How about the kids are with me Monday through Thursday, and we split each weekend? Rashid can have them Fridays and I will have them Saturdays.*

Lisa: *Okay, that's Option B.* [Lisa records that option on the flip chart]

Rashid: *So, I would have the kids one night a week? And not see them for six days in a row? Roberta. Come on. Can we come up with options that aren't ridiculous?*

Kate: *This is a toughy. There are so many factors to consider. I'm wondering if it would feel helpful for Lisa and me to share some scheduling ideas that other families have found work well? Options that many nine-year-olds have done fine with?* [In reality, this intervention would likely come later in the session if the parents got stuck generating their own ideas]

Rashid: [nods]

Roberta: Okay. [crosses her arms and sits back in her chair]

Kate: [jokingly, to Roberta] *Your mouth says "Okay," but I'm not sure what your body's saying.*

Roberta: [smiles and relaxes. Everyone giggles] *Okay, go ahead.*

Lisa: Well, based on what Sue said about the twins being healthy and resilient, I think any of these might work. But you both will need to figure out which ones feel right for your family. [On the flip chart, she sketches out calendars showing a 2-2-5 schedule, a 2-2-3 schedule, one in which Dad has every other weekend from Thursday to Monday morning and one in which Dad has every other weekend from Thursday to Monday plus Thursday overnight on the off week]

[**Kate and Lisa** now talk through what Lisa has written down, explaining how each rhythm might work and some of the advantages and disadvantages of each]

Roberta: Well, Option C [alternate Thursday through Monday morning for Rashid] *has potential. But Sunday is a school night. I would prefer the kids come home to me Sunday night so I can get them ready for school.*

Rashid: That just isn't enough time. I'm not going to agree to that, Roberta. And I resent your suggestion that your house is the kids' only home. I'm not going to let you dole out time for me to be with my children. We both get to decide.

Kate: I know it's hard to look at all these ideas and sit with the anxiety about the options you don't like. But it's true—this process is a two-way street, and, in the end, your parenting plan will need to be something you both feel comfortable with. Lisa—thoughts?

Lisa: You know, we were doing pretty well with brainstorming before. We can get back to that . . . or maybe the two of you would find it helpful to hear a bit about what the research says about schedules for children at this age? I know Roberta is very worried about potential damage to the twins from going back and forth. And Sue offered some reassuring information about how adaptive both of the kids are, and how much they love being with each of you. Perhaps this would be a good time to talk about what mental health professionals look for in a good weekly schedule for kids in general. What do you both think?

[Both parents nod]

[**Lisa and Kate** then review some of the pertinent research data, highlighting the need for frequent and regular access to both parents, the importance of predictability, and the essential role each parent plays in the healthy development of children. They note the challenge of balancing frequency of visits with avoiding too much back-and-forth. They are careful not to advocate any particular schedule, but emphasize the wide range of options that children can generally manage. They also note how important it is that each parent has the opportunity to be involved in the whole range of parenting activities—schooling, social lives, extracurricular activities, morning and evening routines, and weekend downtime.]

Rashid: That all makes a lot of sense. I really want to be able to help the kids with homework sometimes. Malik loves going over spelling words with me before his Friday spelling tests. I don't want to miss that.

Kate: So it might be nice for both you and Malik to have Thursday nights together. How might you accomplish some one-on-one time for the twins? That was something Sue mentioned that you both thought made a lot of sense.

Roberta: Well, let's look at some more options. I'd be willing to consider maybe having the kids split up on Thursday nights—so every other week each twin could have some one-on-one time with each of us.

Lisa: That's a great idea, Roberta. Let's put some more ideas up on the flip chart.

THE DEBRIEF

If you go back to review the last two discussions with Rashid and Roberta, you will recognize some by now familiar techniques. We each made special efforts to empathize with the *other's* client, and to appear neutral in our concern for the whole family. We encouraged each client to express their underlying interests as a way of letting go of strongly held positions. Though Roberta seems to be the more rigid of the two clients, she is not so brittle that she could not soften when offered empathy and understanding. When she felt reassured that both coaches were tuned in to her worry and sense of unfairness, she was able to let go of some of her positions and think more rationally.

We again looked to one another, each making opportunities for the other to step in or taking the initiative when we saw a need. We used our own knowledge from other cases, invoked the research, and called on the input of the child specialist, both to educate the clients and to stretch their thinking. This repeated use of other resources also helped us to refocus the conversation on the interests of the children. Still, we were careful about whether and when to offer our own ideas, wanting to leave adequate time and space for the clients to come up with their own options when they could. When the clients began thinking creatively, both of us encouraged them to continue their own thought process.

We also tried to stay "in the moment," commenting not only on the statements each parent made but also on their nonverbal communication. When Kate lightly noted the contrast between Roberta's words and her body language, the whole group relaxed. Overall, we tried to stay close to where the clients were emotionally, and were careful not to push either client too hard or ask too much of them.

While Rashid may have grown impatient if the weekly schedule did not get resolved within a few meetings, Lisa could have spoken with him about the need for patience in the light of Roberta's distress about the divorce itself. Lisa could also have worked with Rashid to acknowledge that his history of working late and being home little had taken a real toll on Roberta and on his relationship with his children. Lisa and Rashid's attorney could have helped Rashid see the need, perhaps, of an interim or phased-in schedule. At the same time, Kate and Roberta's attorney could have helped Roberta come to terms with the idea that her children needed a fully engaged father, and that four nights a month with Rashid was not going to be enough for them.

After a few meetings with this couple it became clear to us that the themes of the parenting plan would involve Roberta's resistance to seeing herself as a true co-parent (rather than as the "primary" parent), and Rashid's impatience to have the children half-time right away. We knew that the plan would have to take into account Rashid's need for a learning curve (he had never before had to manage the day-to-day lives of his children), as well as time for Roberta to adjust gradually to a new status quo. The dynamic between the parents of Rashid pushing for more and Roberta holding him off would likely weave through almost every discussion of every clause of the plan. If we were to help these parents reach a successful outcome, we were going to have to help them to strike a balance between their conflicting wishes. Their Agreement would not be durable if it included too many restrictions on Rashid, but Roberta would not be able to tolerate the process if we moved too quickly. A successful plan would evolve gradually, and ultimately result in a sensible balance of time for each parent to have full relationships with the twins.

▼▼▼▼▼

Tasks for Collaborative Professionals Helping Clients to Craft a Parenting Plan: An Overview

- Help clients to separate their own needs and anxieties from those of their children.
- Help clients to separate out genuine concerns about a proposed option from the desire to punish the other by reflexively saying "no."
- Help clients to separate genuine concern over the other's parenting capacity from anger or hurt relating to the marital dynamics.
- Help clients to move away from concerns about the other parent as a *partner* from concerns about the other parent as a *parent*.
- Help clients to deal with their grief and fear over giving up time with their children.
- Help clients to imagine a future in which they can not only tolerate but begin to enjoy time away from their children.

- Help the historically "primary" parent work through resentment over giving up sole control of all parenting responsibilities while respecting the learning curve of the other parent.
- Help clients to focus on the psychological experience of their children.
- Help the impatient spouse to tolerate and recognize the importance of respecting the slower pace of the more actively grieving spouse.

FINAL THOUGHTS ON PARENTING PLANNING

The hours we've spent helping couples to craft parenting plans they can feel proud of and that will stand the test of time have been some of the most satisfying we've spent as Collaborative professionals. Nothing is more important to almost all parents than their children, and most parents enter this phase of the process feeling as though they are standing on the edge of a precipice—about to be pushed into an unimaginable abyss. The opportunity to intervene at this moment and, when things go well, to help parents move out of self-focused despair into a child-focused hopefulness is a privilege. Along the way this can be frustrating, hard work. But accompanying parents on this journey is intensely rewarding.

CONCLUSION

This is an exciting time for the Collaborative community. As professionals the world over hear about this way of working, Collaborative training organizations are multiplying, practice groups are expanding and proliferating, and clients are beginning to come through our doors with the express desire to learn more about Collaborative Practice.

Since 1990 when Stu Webb introduced the Collaborative model, professionals have been experimenting with new ways of working together to improve our capacity to meet needs of our clients and their families. Pauline Tesler and Peggy Thompson moved the ball forward by leaps and bounds with their introduction of the multidisciplinary team model and their focus on the psychological dimensions of our work. More professionals are employing the Collaborative model to resolve civil disputes; in fact, the training organization in which we teach (CPTI) now addresses the application of Collaborative Practice protocols in the non-divorce legal arena in our Introductory Multidisciplinary Three-Day Training. And important new ideas are cropping up all the time. One of the most promising frontiers is the intersection of Collaborative Practice and neuroscience. This area of exploration will no doubt exert an increasing influence over all of us.

As we've said, Collaborative doesn't mean easy. Like any professional community, ours has its tensions and challenges. As advocates of Collaborative Practice we each have an investment in the general well-being and expansion of the field. We want to work to raise standards of practice and increase the public's awareness of and access to Collaborative professionals. So we are eager to invite new colleagues into the community, refer them to training programs, and help them to get up and running as competent Collaborative practitioners. On the other hand, we often find ourselves opting to work with familiar colleagues. A team that thinks and works smoothly together and is characterized by mutual trust and respect is worth its weight in gold. Striking a balance between taking chances on new teammates and sticking with the tried and true is an ongoing challenge for many of us.

And there are other challenges. Knowing that a colleague may benefit from negative feedback while worrying that such honesty might sour a relationship is a familiar sticky wicket. After all, relationships with team members often generate referrals, may extend into the future on new cases, and must survive in the greater community of practice group meetings, social gatherings, and training programs. Choosing to have a difficult conversation can sometimes seem the harder road. Yet those conversations are often crucial, not only for the recipient of our ideas and the quality of our Collaborative work, but in preserving our own professional integrity. If we choose not to have the tough talk, our frustration with a fellow practitioner is likely to find expression in unhelpful ways. The authors' wake-up call came when, after we had allowed ourselves to indulge in a gossip session with colleagues, one of them astutely commented, "This doesn't feel very *Collaborative* to me."

Ours is hard work. It requires not only a depth of professional experience, but a special blend of personal characteristics. These include self-awareness, non-defensive openness to feedback, the ability to work effectively on teams, the capacity to connect with others, an appreciation of varying perspectives, the ability to think creatively on your feet, energy, and self-confidence. While there is room in the field for a wide range of personalities (in fact, working with colleagues who have differing styles is part of the richness of the experience), this is not a job for shrinking violets. Team members and clients rely on us to pull our weight in a case, as well as to remain emotionally present and to speak up at meetings. While everyone will forgive us a mistake, they will quickly come to resent us if we don't fully participate. If we are at the Collaborative table and we don't add something, we are subtracting.

The authors are lucky in that we have often experienced the magic of working cohesively with gifted teammates. Whether we are working with an inherently collaborative couple or clients who cause us to momentarily question our career choice, one thing remains true: the more closely attuned we stay to the emotional undercurrents in the room, the better our work will be. In this book we've taken many of the concepts we've learned over the last 20 years in the mental health field, synthesized them, and reshaped them into new models. The result is a theoretical framework that we've found useful for understanding our clients, our teams, and ourselves, for tailoring interventions to the strengths and vulnerabilities of each client, and for improving our capacities at the Collaborative table.

To revisit the our opening metaphor: we hope that by reading this book you'll have come to appreciate the value of paying attention to what lies below the surface of our Collaborative work, and that you'll have gained some tools for understanding and navigating this new terrain. We wish you many richly rewarding journeys down the Collaborative river.

REFERENCES

Constance Ahrons, *The Good Divorce* (Harper Paperbacks, 1998).

W. Bion, *Experiences in Groups* (Basic Books, 1961).

W.R.D. Fairbairn, "Endopsychic Structure Considered in Terms of Object Relationships," in *Psychoanalytic Studies of the Personality* (Routledge and Kegan Paul, 1952), 82–135.

Roger Fisher, William Ury, and Bruce Patton, *Getting to Yes: Negotiating Agreement Without Giving In* (Penguin, 1991).

Anna Freud, *The Ego and the Mechanisms of Defense* (International Universities Press, 1946).

Atul Gawande, *The Checklist Manifesto: How to Get Things Right* (Metropolitan Books, 2009).

Janet Johnston, Vivienne Roseby, and Kathryn Kuehnle, *In the Name of the Child* (Springer Publishing, 2009).

M. Klein, "Notes on Some Schizoid Mechanisms," *International Journal of Psycho-Analysis* 27:99–100.

Robert Mnookin, *Bargaining with the Devil: When to Negotiate, When to Fight* (Simon and Schuster, 2010).

Ron Ousky and Stuart Webb, *The Collaborative Way to Divorce: The Revolutionary Method That Results in Less Stress, Lower Costs, and Happier Kids—Without Going to Court* (Hudson Street Press, 2006).

David E. Scharff and Jill S. Scharff, *New Paradigms for Treating Relationships* (Jason Aronson, 2006).

David E. Scharff and Jill S. Scharff, *Object Relations Couple Therapy* (Jason Aronson, 1991).

David Scharff and Jill Scharff, *Scharff Notes: A Primer of Object Relations Therapy* (Jason Aronson, 1992).

Kate Scharff, *Therapy Demystified: An Insider's Guide to Getting the Right Help (Without Going Broke)* (Marlowe and Co., 2004).

Douglas Stone, Bruce Patton, and Sheila Heen, *Difficult Conversations: How to Discuss What Matters Most* (Penguin Books, 2000).

Pauline Tesler, *Collaborative Law: Achieving Effective Resolution in Divorce Without Litigation*, 2nd ed. (American Bar Association, 2008).

Pauline Tesler and Peggy Thompson, *Collaborative Divorce: The Revolutionary New Way to Restructure Your Family, Resolve Legal Issues, and Move On with Your Life* (ReganBooks/Harper Collins, 2006).

William L. Ury, *Getting Past No: Negotiating in Difficult Situations* (Bantam, 1993)

William L. Ury, *Getting to Yes* (see above under Fisher).

Anne "Jan" White, Susan Butler, Betsey J. Case, Marge Coffey, Ali Doyle, Karen Freed, Marjorie Just, Anne Lopiano, Debbie May, Daniel Renart, Paul Smollar, Sue Soler, and Sarah Zimmerman, *Best Practice Protocol Resources for a Full Team Model: Collaborative Divorce*, Jan. 2010 (unpublished at the time of this writing).

INDEX